D0569710

A GUIDE TO

THE DOCUMENTATION OF

PSYCHOLOGY

A GUIDE TO

THE DOCUMENTATION OF

PSYCHOLOGY

C K ELLIOTT BA PhD

Senior Lecturer in Psychology
University of Bradford Management Centre

LINNET BOOKS & CLIVE BINGLEY

FIRST PUBLISHED 1971 BY CLIVE BINGLEY LTD
THIS EDITION SIMULTANEOUSLY PUBLISHED IN THE USA
BY LINNET BOOKS, AN IMPRINT OF SHOE STRING PRESS INC,
995 SHERMAN AVENUE, HAMDEN, CONNECTICUT 06514
PRINTED IN GREAT BRITAIN
COPYRIGHT © C K ELLIOTT 1971
ALL RIGHTS RESERVED
0–208–01072–6

CONTENTS

5

Figures

PREFACE

This book is intended as a simple guide to the current documentation of psychology, and as a reference source to some of the more common materials. It will be of most use to the advanced undergraduate and first year postgraduate student conducting research into psychology and related subjects. Psychologists, in common with other scientists, are increasingly being required to assimilate and use more and more information, but many are not aware of the facilities available to help them. The present book had its origins in my courses in research methods. Even the most elementary research project calls for a combination of many skills. Some of these, such as survey and experimental methods and statistical computation, are well served by textbooks, but students are often expected to be proficient in documentary skills without being offered any training. My experience indicates that all students benefit from some formal instruction in documentation. This should not be seen as an attempt to turn them into novice librarians, but to teach them sufficient of the techniques so that they know what questions to ask the qualified librarian. This book will be of little value to the historian of psychology, as only currently available materials are given. The historian is referred to Louttit, C M *Handbook of psychological literature*, Principia Press 1932, and Daniel, R S and Louttit, C M *Professional problems in psychology*, Prentice Hall 1953. Librarians will be horrified by the over simplification of their procedures in the body of the book, but I hope that the appendices may be of some use to those who have to deal with psychology.

Chapter 1 is an introduction to psychology and an indication of what I regard as related subjects, mainly for the reader who is not a qualified psychologist, but who has to deal with psychological topics. Chapter 2 is an introduction to libraries and classification systems. Chapter 3 considers why the research worker should be interested in documentation, and outlines some uses of information. Chapter 4 presents some of the tools which can be used to tackle information problems. Where there are only a few relevant tools in any category, they are listed in chapter 4; but more extensive categories are listed in appendices. The next three chapters consider 'how to do it': the comprehensive search, current awareness and everyday reference. It must be stressed that there can be no single 'best way' and so the methods given merely represent some products of my experience. The final chapter contains a miscellany of topics which are relevant to documentation problems, but which do not conveniently fit elsewhere in the book.

Different criteria were used for the inclusion of material in the various appendices. In general, secondary sources were included even when they were considered marginally related to psychology, so that the reader may locate primary information from a wide range of sources. A narrower view was taken of journals (in appendix B) and only those were included which I considered to be the central core of psychology, because of the sheer magnitude of the task. The key-word in context layout for appendices E and F was influenced by the similar format indexes produced by the National Lending Library. The indexes for this book were produced independently, however, and contain foreign language sources whereas the NLL indexes concentrate upon their holdings of English language material.

Many influences contributed to this book. Many librarians have most willingly given up their time to instruct me in their professional skills. Neil Hunter, University of Bradford Management Centre Librarian, read the early drafts and suggested modifications and additional material. J M Brittain was one of the few psychologists interested in documentation problems who suggested changes after reading the first draft. Dr J Hoskovec supplied information about several of the dictionaries in appendices H and I; and details of British organisations connected with psychology in appendix A were supplied by F H Partridge, Executive Secretary of the British Psychological Society. Mrs Barbara McAlpine checked the bibliographic references in appendices G, H and I, and the manuscript was typed by Miss Judith Clough.

Parts of chapters 2 and 4 are an extension of my paper: 'The documentation of psychology' in the *Bulletin of the British Psychological Society*, reproduced here with the permission of the British Psychological Society. Figure 5 is reproduced from *Education index* with the permission of the H W Wilson Company; figure 6 from *Perceptual cognitive development* (the Galton Institute); figure 7 from *Science citation index* (Institute for Scientific Information) and figure 8 from *Psychological abstracts* (American Psychological Association).

CHAPTER 1

PSYCHOLOGY AND RELATED SUBJECTS

THE NATURE OF PSYCHOLOGY

Psychology may be briefly defined as the scientific study of human and animal behaviour. This definition stresses three aspects of psychology. It is scientific in that methods of empirical enquiry are used to obtain data, rather than introspection and armchair speculation; the subject matter is observable behaviour and those necessary constructs, such as intelligence, which are operationally tied to observable behaviour; and animal as well as human behaviour is of interest, because it is generally the process, such as learning, perception, motivation, rather than the behaving organism, that is of prime importance.

Two approaches to this subject matter can be distinguished. One approach focuses on the components or processes common to any behavioural act. All behaviour involves to a greater or lesser degree aspects of learning, perception, motivation, emotion, etc and psychological science attempts to develop theories and to explain and predict these acts, whilst ignoring differences between individuals. The second approach concentrates upon these differences, primarily but not exclusively, in humans, and uses concepts such as intelligence and abilities, attitudes and personality to describe and explain such differences.

RELATED SUBJECTS

It is difficult, if not impossible, to draw rigid boundaries which mark off the limits of any science. The diagram in figure 1 shows some of the relationships between psychology and related topics, and indicate some of the sub-specialisms within psychology. Figure 1 should be multi-dimensional, however, because there are also influences within and amongst the ' related subjects ' and so the diagram indicates an essentially psychocentric universe.

These relationships have substantial implications for the use of documentation. The literature of psychology is widely scattered, and thus psychologists are likely to consult and contribute to material in a very wide range of sources. For example, Daniel ' Psychology ' *Library trends,* 1967 *15* (4), pages 670-684, reported that twenty

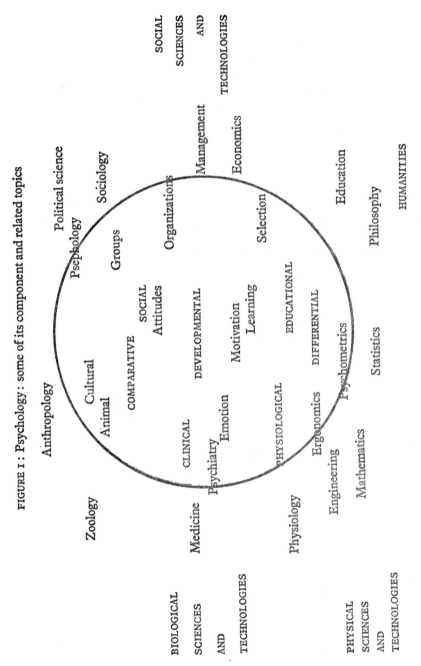

FIGURE I : Psychology : some of its component and related topics

psychological journals contained references to 660 other journals. For further evidence of scattering *see* Brittain *Information and its users* (1970, pages 139-143). In this book I have attempted to indicate some of the more likely common sources, but these cannot be regarded as exhaustive. Four major spheres of influence are shown in figure 1. Psychology as a behavioural or social science has obvious links with other behavioural sciences. The strongest link is with sociology, giving the boundary zone of social psychology which is particularly concerned with group structure and function, and social influences upon individual behaviour as shown by attitudes, prejudice and the use of language. The links with other social sciences are less strong but, for example, the psychologist shares an interest with the political scientist in psephology (the study of voting), with the economist in buyer behaviour and such phenomena as fashion, and with the anthropologist in studying cultural and racial differences in intelligence and personality. As well as having links with social sciences, psychology also contributes to social technologies in which the scientific knowledge of the social sciences is applied. These include social work, market research, education, and management.

Psychology also has strong links with the biological sciences. This is particularly true in the case of physiology, where the boundary zone known as physiological psychology is particularly concerned with the study of sensation and perception, with neurology in understanding the brain structures responsible for specific behaviours, and with zoology in comparative animal psychology and ethology. The technologies based on the biological sciences also receive contributions from psychology and contribute to psychological knowledge. This is particularly the case in medicine and especially in psychiatry. Clinical psychologists engage in both diagnostic and therapeutic work. Psychoanalysis is difficult to locate exactly, because from one point of view it can be seen as a branch of psychiatry, but from another it is a wide ranging theory of personality which has contributed to our understanding of motivation, perception and child development.

Psychology has links with the humanities, particularly with philosophy. The award of the doctorate in philosophy as the higher degree in all branches of knowledge is an acknowledgement of the descent of all science from philosophy. In the case of psychology though, the separation is relatively recent. This is shown in library classification

13

schemes such as Dewey which present psychology as a branch of philosophy (*see* chapter 2). The philosophers' tools, such as linguistic analysis, are useful for the psychologist when he has to use everyday expressions such as intelligence in a specialised sense. The analysis of such concepts has given rise to a field of philosophical psychology.

Fourthly, psychology has links with the natural sciences. This is particularly found with mathematics where a branch of mathematical psychology is a recent development. The technologies based upon the natural sciences also contribute to psychology and again receive contributions from psychology. Statistical techniques are necessary in the evaluation of experimental data, and the problems peculiar to data used in psychology led to the development of psychometrics and psychophysics. Specialist statistical techniques such as correlation, factor analysis and non-metric scaling, which were developed in these areas, are now widely used in all branches of statistics. Engineering has strong links with psychology in ergonomics or human engineering; the study of the interaction of man, machine, and environment.

It can be seen that psychology caters for a wide range of taste amongst its adherents: for some the hope of helping others may be a prime motive, whereas for others it is the chance to develop further a science which offers unique challenges.

PSYCHOLOGICAL RESEARCH

Because of its relative newness as an independent discipline there is a high ratio of research workers to appliers of existing knowledge. Although there is still room for the lone research worker, most new advances in psychological knowledge tend to come from workers and teams based in universities, research organisations, government departments, large clinics and hospitals. Details of university departments of psychology can be found in the *World of learning* and the *Commonwealth universities yearbook,* and news of individual departments of psychology throughout the world is given in the *International journal of psychology.* Research organisations may be located through the *European research index* (second edition) Francis Hodgson Ltd, and the American *Research centers directory* (second edition) Gale Research Co.

The vast bulk of research work in psychology is undertaken in the United States, with the rest of the world lagging some way behind.

Details of graduate study programmes in over 300 United States and Canadian universities are given in *Graduate study in psychology,* American Psychological Association. International comparisons of psychological training and research are made by Ross, S, Alexander, I, Basowitz, H, Werber, M, and Nicholas, P in *International opportunities for advanced training and research in psychology* (American Psychological Association, 1966, 395 pages). Information about the educational system, advanced psychological training and research both in and outside universities, recognition and the legal status of psychology, prospects for international exchanges and bibliographic sources are given for eighty seven countries. A similar study, giving details of the training and status of clinical psychology in fifty eight countries, is David, H P *International resources in clinical psychology* (McGraw-Hill, 1964, 236 pages). A survey of developments in British psychology was produced as a special supplement to the *Bulletin of the British Pcychological Society* on the occasion of the nineteenth International Congress of Psychology (Foss, B M *ed Psychology in Great Britain,* British Psychological Society, 1969, 48 pages); this publication also gives a list of previous International Congresses of Psychology and details of the published proceedings.

The publications of psychologists in Western European countries are reasonably accessible to English speaking psychologists, but language difficulties restrict Oriental and Russian research from all but a very limited readership. The *Annual review of psychology* has attempted to bridge this gap by publishing a series of articles on Soviet and Japanese psychology. The most recent are: Brozek, ' Recent developments in Soviet psychology ' in the *Annual review of psychology,* 1964 *15,* pages 493-594, and Tanaka, ' Status of Japanese experimental psychology ' in the *Annual review of psychology,* 1966 *17,* pages 233-272. Several English language journals devoted to making this information more accessible are given in appendix C.

SUPPORT FOR PSYCHOLOGICAL RESEARCH

Three major sources of public funds support psychological research in Britain. The Science Research Council covers the biological aspects of the subject including the experimental study of human behaviour, and the Social Science Research Council covers the remainder. Medical Research Council support is much wider than its title would indicate and work in most areas, both pure and applied, is supported. Details are given in the *Social Science Research Council newsletter* no 9, June 1970. This pattern of public support may be compared with that in the United States from information given in *American behavioural scientist*, 1964 7 (5) and *American psychologist*, 1969 24, pages 691-694.

The sponsorship of research is likely to have an influence upon the publication and availability of results. Research privately sponsored by firms is unlikely to be published openly until sufficient time has elapsed to avoid the possibility of competitors gaining from the knowledge, and government research may be security classified. On the other hand, however, it is often a requirement that researchers in receipt of public funds publish their results openly. Thus reports of research supported by the Social Science Research Council are freely available from the National Lending Library, and data for secondary analysis are held in the SSRC data bank at the University of Essex.

PSYCHOLOGICAL ORGANISATIONS

Two international psychological societies hold regular congresses and co-ordinate the activities of national societies. The *International journal of psychology* is the organ of the International Union of Scientific Psychology (IUSP), and the *International review of applied psychology* the organ of the International Association of Applied Psychology (IAAP). National societies exist in most advanced countries and up to date details of these can be found annually in part 1 of the *International journal of psychology* (details of thirty six national societies were given in the *International journal of psychology* 1970, 5, pages 43-46). Other international organisations having considerable links with psychology are the World Federation for Mental Health and the International Biological Programme. Information about various national social councils was given in *Social science information*, volume 8.

In Britain the major organisation for psychologists is the British Psychological Society while the Experimental Psychology Society exists to further the interests of a limited group of psychological researchers. The British Association for the Advancement of Science has a Psychology Section (Section J). Details of other organisations related to psychology are given in appendix A.

CHAPTER 2

LIBRARIES AND CLASSIFICATION

A library is best considered as a store of information rather than a collection of books. The format of the information has changed in the past (from handwritten manuscript to printed document), and is currently changing again (with the increase in micro-format material and computer storage of information).

Four different types of libraries which fulfil different functions may be distinguished. National libraries are state institutions supported wholly or largely from government funds. In Britain the British Museum Library is the major national library, and others include the National Library of Scotland, the Science Museum Library and the Library of the National History Museum. The National Central Library is a major source of books for interlibrary loan services. Two relatively recent developments have been the National Lending Library for Science and Technology which acts to supplement the holdings of journals for all other libraries, and the National Reference Library for Science and Invention as an offshoot of the British Museum Library. With the exception of the National Lending Library and the National Central Library, the main role of national libraries is not to lend material but to preserve it, to act as reference libraries and sometimes to provide a bibliographic service. In order to provide a store of all items published in Britain the Copyright Acts require all publishers to deposit copies of each publication in six copyright privilege libraries, including the British Museum.

Public libraries are administered by local government authorities and supported from the rates. They mainly lend books for home reading, and many now also lend gramophone records, films and other audio-visual aids, original paintings and reproductions. Most large city libraries include a commercial and technical library which provides a service to local industry. The larger branch libraries operate enquiry services and have reference sections, but this division into lending and reference should not obscure the fact that important reference material may be available in the lending section. Any book containing an index may be considered as a potential reference aid.

Because of the large numbers of books being published, a national subject specialisation scheme has been introduced to ensure that every book in the *British national bibliography* (BNB) can be located somewhere in the country. For example, the Yorkshire regional library system is responsible for classes 300 to 349 in BNB. For details of the services offered by public libraries *see The public library service today* reports on education no 57, July 1969.

The extent of the stocks found in a university library is often directly related to its age. Details of universities and their libraries, including any special collections, can be obtained from the *Commonwealth universities yearbook, American universities and colleges* and *International handbook of universities*. Some indication of the size of the psychology section can be gained from information given in these handbooks about the extent of the teaching staff in psychology.

Special libraries are devoted to the literature of a special subject or group of subjects. They are not generally open to the public, but exist for the members of learned societies, or the staff of government departments, research organisations and large firms. They frequently operate information services to exploit the information within their specialist field and normally lend material to other libraries. Some libraries specialise in non-book material, for example the national audio-visual aids library. Classified details of all types of special libraries and national, regional and local cooperative schemes in Great Britain are given in Wilson, B J (*ed*), *ASLIB directory* (2 vols), London: Aslib 1970.

CLASSIFICATION

Information in a store is only of use if it can be retrieved quickly and accurately when required, and this is facilitated by a classification system. A subject classification attempts to reproduce the classifiers view of the orderliness of the subject matter in the organisation of the documents about that subject matter, so that related subjects are grouped together and separated from unrelated subjects. Psychology is poorly served by most classification schemes, however, because of its multitude of related topics. Many schemes classify it with philosophy and ignore its strong relationship with the biological sciences.

In a hierarchical system the user can be led to related material at a superordinate or subordinate level. For example, an enquiry in a small library for material on vision may yield insufficient material at that level, and the classification system would lead one to look under increasingly superordinate terms such as perception, or psychology. A similar enquiry in a large specialised library would produce too much material, and then the classification system would enable one to refine the enquiry to more specific subordinate terms, such as threshold measurement, dark adaptation, or the Purkinje shift.

Decimal Classification (DC)

This most widely used and best known system was first published by Melvil Dewey in 1876. The current edition is published as Dewey, M *Decimal classification and the relative index* (seventeenth edition), 2 vols, Lake Placid, Forest Press, 1965. It divides the whole of knowledge into ten classes, each class being further subdivided using a decimal notation until the desired level of specificity is reached (see figure 2). A classification number obtained from the schedule may be further specified by the use of ' standard subdivisions '. For example:

the mode of treatment of the subject: 018 research methodology
                                        0186   case studies
the form of the material: 07   study and teaching
                             077   programmed teaching

Thus, case studies of gifted children would be classified as 155.4550186 and a programmed text in industrial psychology as 158.7077.

No classification system intended for the totality of material held by a general library can bring together all the material likely to be of use to the reader, and so the user has to become familiar with those other parts of the system which are likely to contain material of interest. In DC there is no mention of social psychology within the psychology section of the schedule, but it is included under SOCIOLOGY at 301.1; other examples include mental deficiency at 616.8588 under MEDICAL SCIENCES, and performance rating at 658.3125 under MANAGEMENT.

Universal Decimal Classification (UDC)

This was based on the Decimal Classification and originated in a European plan to compile a complete bibliography of all published literature. The bibliography was discontinued in 1918, but the development of classification system has continued. It retains the decimal notation and main class structure of DC, but uses more than one

FIGURE 2: An example of subject hierarchy in the Decimal Classification

000   Generalities
100   Philosophy and related disciplines

.

.

.

140   Specific philosophical viewpoints
150   Psychology
     152   Physiological and experimental psychology
        152·1   Sensory perception
        152·15   Auditory perception
        152·152   Pitch perception

        .

        .

        .

     153   Intelligence
     154   Subconscious states and processes
     155   Differential and genetic
     156   Comparative
     157   Abnormal and clinical
     158   Applied
     159   Other aspects
160   Logic

.

.

.

200   Religion
300   Social sciences
400   Language
500   Pure sciences
600   Technology
700   Arts
800   Literature
900   General geography and history

decimal point to divide up long numbers. UDC first appeared in French, and the English translations are published as *British standard 1000*. In the psychology section (BS 1000 [159.9]) the French parentage can be clearly seen, for example by the attention devoted to GRAPHOLOGY. In addition, some of the section headings are literal translations and rarely used in English (*eg* PSYCHOTECHNIQUE).

The basic number for psychology is 159.9 (*cf* 150 in DC), and therefore very long numbers can be generated:

159.95	HIGHER MENTAL PROCESSES
159.953	MEMORY, LEARNING
159.953.3	MEMORY PROCESSES
159.953.34	REPRODUCTION, REPRESENTATION
159.953.344	TYPES OF STIMULATION FOR EXCITATION OF MEMORY
159.953.344.3	IMAGERY

UDC makes extensive use of ' auxiliaries ' which may be compared with the ' standard subdivisions ' of DC, for example:

:   the document includes related concepts at an equal level, *eg* 159.9:311.16 for correlational methods in psychology. The librarian has to decide whether to shelve the document at 159.9 with other documents on psychology, or at 311.16 with correlational methods.

(0. . .) indicates form of the document *eg* 159.0(058) indicates a yearbook of abnormal psychology.

00. . . indicates point of view *eg* 159.9.001.57 indicates the use of models in psychology.

Special auxiliary subdivisions can be applied to some parts of the scheme to increase the specificity of a classification number derived from the main schedules. Special auxiliary subdivisions are given for ' System and schools ', 'Apparatus ', ' Methods of research ', etc for use within the PSYCHOLOGY main schedule. These auxiliary subdivisions are arranged in hierarchical order like the main schedules:

159.9.07	EXPERIMENTAL PSYCHOLOGY, RESEARCH
159.9.072	TESTS, INVESTIGATIONS
159.9.072.5	METHODS
159.9.072.53	OBJECTIVE METHODS
159.9.072.533	REACTION METHODS
159.9.072.533.8	PSYCHO-GALVANIC METHODS

The combination of main schedule number and auxiliary subdivision number can give rise to a very complex classification. Should a study have been conducted which investigated imagery as excitation for memory using psycho-galvanic methods, the appropriate classification for the report would be: 159.953.344.3.072.533.8.

This demonstrates both the strength and weakness of UDC. A complex classification such as this would be ideal for a specialist information retrieval system, staffed by subject experts highly trained in the use of the system. For book classification in the average library it would be far too detailed, however, and the complex rules which determine the shelving order for books would result in the inability of most users to obtain their requirements. For these reasons, book classification does not usually exploit the full potential of the system.

Library of Congress
This was not intended as a universal system, but was developed to classify the material held by the United States Library of Congress. In view of the size and importance of this collection, however, the system has been considered sufficiently comprehensive for it to be adopted by other national libraries, as well as a number of American university and public libraries. The Library of Congress is organised into subject departments, and so the schedules under each main subject heading were developed by experts in the bibliography of that subject, but independently of other subjects. Each main class is published as a separate schedule; PSYCHOLOGY (BF) is part of the main class of philosophy and religion (class B). The system is not hierarchical and the schedules for psychology are not very detailed, so it throws together heterogeneous material when used with a comprehensive collection. For example, only one undivided location is given for all material on vision (BF 241), and all the variety of statistical methods in psychology are undifferentiated at BF 39. The compilers accept that this is unsatisfactory, and state in the preface: 'In psychology . . . a thoroughgoing revision beyond the limits of the editorial revision embodied in this edition is needed . . .', Library of Congress, subject cataloging division *Classification class B. Part I* (second edition) 1950.

Bliss: Bibliographic Classification
This system is of particular interest to psychologists because the psychology class was compiled in collaboration with C M Louttit, a

psychologist who was a major figure in the development of the bibliography of psychology (*see* Bliss, H E *A bibliographic classification*, vols 1 and 2, second edition. Wilson 1952). The schedules use the letters of the alphabet rather than numbers, and so there is a wider base for the division of knowledge. This results in a shorter classification notation at a given level of specificity when compared with the decimal system. The simplicity of the schedules, combined with the detail of the index, makes it ideal for a classifier who does not have an extensive knowledge of the subject, and so it would be useful for a small departmental library.

For example:

I   PSYCHOLOGY

IG   PERSONALITY, INTELLIGENCE AND MENTAL ABILITIES

IGI   CREATIVE ABILITY, ORIGINALITY

In addition to the main schedules there are systematic auxiliary schedules for form, geography, language, historical periods, etc. Details from these are added to the main classification, *eg* ICL2 is a bibliography (form schedule, 2) of VISUAL PERCEPTION (main schedule, ICL).

Every classification system is a product of the prevailing view of the world at the time of its origination. Thus the Decimal Classification interred psychology with the occult and logic, which was probably reasonable in view of the development of psychology in 1876. A Marxist-Leninist view of psychology is given in Khandzhyan, I G, *Bibliotechnobibliograficheskaya klassifikatsiya . . . XXIII Yu. Filosofskie nauki. Psikhologiya* (Bibliographic classification for libraries, volume XXIII, section Yu. Philosophical sciences, Psychology, pages 125-208) Moscow, Kniga, 1967.

The problems of the classification of the social science literature are reviewed by Brittain *Information and its users* (pages 54-63), and evaluated in an editorial introduction to the *Mental health book review index* number 15 (1965).

CATALOGUES

It is necessary to refer to the catalogue of the library to locate a specific item and to discover the extent of material held on any subject. Browsing amongst the shelves is a very inadequate way of finding information, as this will only reveal material that is not currently in use.

A catalogue attempts to cater for the various approaches to the information which the searcher may take. The most common approaches are by author (or editor, translator, collaborator, etc), by title, or by subject, but alternative approaches are possible via names of series, serials where the name of the editor is likely to change from time to time, symposia or conference proceedings. In addition to personal authors, an author approach may be possible via societies, such as American Psychological Association, corporate bodies (universities, firms, etc), government departments (Great Britain, Ministry of . . .), international organisations (International Association for . . .).

Two main types of catalogue are found. The ' dictionary catalogue ' which is widely used in the US brings together in one sequence the author, title and subject entries. The alternative system in general use in the UK has three separate sequences. The author catalogue is particularly used for locating a specific item when the author is known. The classified subject catalogue indicates the extent of material on specific subjects by bringing together all the entries classified together. It is therefore in the same order as the material on the shelves, but of course the cards are always there, whereas the books may be away on loan. The alphabetical subject index provides a key to the classified subject catalogue by giving the classification identification for all subjects covered by the library.

Consistency in the description of material entered and the order of entry in catalogues from library to library are ensured by the use of an international code of practice (*Anglo-American cataloguing rules,* London, the Library Association 1967, 327 pages). Two types of alphabetical filing order are in common use. In a ' letter-by-letter ' arrangement the spaces between words in an entry are ignored, whereas in a ' word-by-word ' arrangement each word is treated separately to determine the alphabetical order. These two methods result in substantial differences in order, as shown in the following examples :

Letter-by-letter	*Word-by-word*
rat breeding (genetics)	rat breeding (genetics)
rate control	rat maze
rating scales	rate control
rationalization	rating scales
rat maze	rationalization

Where a word with identical spelling can be a person, a place, a title, or a subject, the conventional order is person, place, subject (other than a person or place), title.

The earliest library catalogues were in book form, but because of the difficulty of inserting additional entries the use of card and sheaf catalogues developed. Library 'housekeeping' routines are now increasingly being taken over by the computer and this is enabling a reversion to the earlier practice. A computer can store all the catalogue details and print out complete book-form catalogues or supplements whenever updated editions are necessary. Centralised cataloguing is also being developed helped by services such as the British National Bibliography MARC tapes which provide bibliographical details in machine readable form.

CHAPTER 3

FUNCTIONS OF INFORMATION

A mark of the educated person is not the possession of encyclopedic knowledge but the ability to find relevant information. In the early days of science it was possible for any practitioner to remember most of the information needed in his everyday work, but with the expansion of all fields of knowledge such a situation is now neither possible nor desirable. The various functions of information in the professional life of a scientist are considered in this chapter.

All research scientists use three types of information which may be labelled conceptual, empirical and procedural. Conceptual information involves ideas and takes the form of scientific hypotheses and the collection of verified hypotheses into theories or laws. Empirical information involves facts as the raw material of science. Although there is plentiful scope for philosophers to dispute the status of a ' fact ', there is general agreement amongst scientists that some details may be regarded as basic. As a relatively young empirical science, psychology does not have the same wealth of empirical information as chemistry, for example, but there is a body of generally agreed data on human behaviour as evidenced by handbooks such as Stevens *Handbook of experimental psychology* and Berelson and Steiner *Human behavior: an inventory of scientific findings (see* appendix G). Procedural information concerns methods of scientific investigation. The multiplicity of such methods is one reason why the scientist has to serve an apprenticeship under the detailed supervision of a qualified master. In psychology procedural information spans a wide spectrum from logical operation for the generation of testable hypotheses to the techniques of handling laboratory animals and the manipulation of statistical data. A fourth category of stimulating information is sometimes distinguished. This does not imply that conceptual, empirical or procedural information cannot in itself be stimulating, but that there is a class of information which is not concerned solely with these three former categories but is devoted to the incitement of scientific curiosity. Such information acts to stimulate the individual to participate in scientific endeavour by showing unsolved problems or practical needs of society.

26

Stimulating information may take many forms, both oral and printed (ranging from newspaper reports to scholarly reviews of research in progress). Many scientists report that one result of attending conferences is an emotional stimulation together with an increased self-confidence and determination. This is often not specific to any particular aspect of work but refers to scientific work generally. The stimulating character of information often depends as much on the mental attitude of the receiver as upon the style and format of the information.

This threefold categorisation of information is not rigid since new concepts often require new procedures and lead to new facts which in turn lead to a further generation of new concepts; empirical data can only be properly evaluated after considering its conceptual basis and method of collection. The distinction is useful, however, as different types of information are required at different stages in a research project. Conceptual information is mainly needed at the outset when research is proceeding from the vague awareness of a problem towards the development of a specific hypothesis and later when conclusions are being formulated. Empirical and procedural information are mainly sought after the hypothesis has been specified but before starting research intended to verify it. Many publications tend to specialise in presenting one of these types of information; for example, *Psychological review* is predominantly conceptual and *Psychological bulletin* procedural.

Scientific information may be regarded from another viewpoint, that of its use. Three distinct yet overlapping uses of information may be distinguished. A comprehensive search conducted prior to empirical research involves the most extensive use of information when the searcher attempts to find as much as possible related to the research topic. Literature searching is rarely an end in itself for the scientist, but a means to the end of satisfactory empirical research. The literature search can never be complete because there is always the possibility of information of value being contained in out-of-the-way publications and in foreign languages which the searcher does not read. New information is also continually being created, and so the scientist must at some point call a halt to the preliminary literature search and get on with the empirical investigation. Suggested routines for the comprehensive search are given in chaper 5.

Current awareness can be considered as the continuation into the future of the retrospective literature search. Current awareness is thus a routine task for all scientists and involves keeping up to date with all types of new information. During the development stage a research project may be modified or redesigned as a replication of recently published findings found by current awareness routines. Changes at this stage can avert the later problem of being refused publication because of the earlier findings. Generalisations from apparently remote topics may shed new light upon the project. For example, a colleague was able to develop a novel angle on factory labour turnover by extrapolating theoretical work from anthropology on the relationship between geographical mobility and kinship. During empirical work, awareness of published findings may suggest further analyses of data already collected. *Post-hoc* comparisons and other ' data snooping ' techniques can be employed to check whether these results support reported findings. Clues about the development of other research will help the decision whether to stake a claim by publishing preliminary findings or delay publication until complete results are ready. Some current awareness techniques are given in chapter 6.

Everyday reference involves finding answers to specific questions, and information will be sought from the most accessible reliable source. The dividing line between everyday reference questions and comprehensive searches is not completely distinct, since there can be dispute about apparent facts and attempts to resolve these disputes may involve extensive searching. The everyday reference question implies, however, that the questioner believes that the answer is available, and may only involve refreshing his memory, whereas comprehensive search and current awareness represent more an exploration of the unknown. Some examples of everyday reference questions are given in chapter 7.

The three main uses of conceptual, empirical and procedural information give rise to nine different kinds of information request, examples of which are shown in figure 3. This tabulation is intended to help the user to focus upon that aspect of information in which he is interested, thus resulting in questions which will be precise and therefore more likely to be soluble. Scientists are often dissatisfied with the information provided them by a library, possibly because they ask the wrong kind of question. Librarians for their part frequently find that scientists do not ask for the specific information they

FIGURE 3 : Kinds of requests for information

TYPE OF INFORMATION

USES	Conceptual	Empirical	Procedural
Comprehensive search	eg All the theories about the cause of neurosis	eg All the data on the relationship of material deprivation and neurosis	eg All the methods of measuring anxiety
Current awareness	eg What new ideas in the field of behaviour therapy	eg What are the latest data on social class and hysteria	eg What new methods of electronic recording of physiological functioning
Everyday reference	eg How did Masserman 'cure' experimental neurosis in cats	eg What are the norms for the EPI neuroticism scale	eg How to measure anxiety by polygraph.

really want but ask a general question such as 'have you anything about . . .?'. Instead of the researcher at the outset saying that he wanted to know everything about schizophrenia, or the learning ability of the white rat, or the human ageing process, he should specify which ideas, facts, or methods of enquiry are his prime requirements.

Contained within the three main uses of information are several categories which may be considered independently in other circumstances. Research scientists must specialise, but additionally they need to keep themselves informed of progress in secondary areas. Areas may be secondary because of the amount of information which is sought—only details of results and not methods—or the use to which the information is to be put, for example, teaching or supervision of other research workers. It is frequently necessary to review recent work in these secondary areas. For example, the psychologist working on perception may need a quick review of central nervous system depressants if a theory of perception hinges upon an analogy with brain chemistry. In this situation he is not interested in this information in the same manner as would be a biochemist, but will want more than the beginning student in biochemistry. So a textbook would be of limited use, but handbooks and review articles may provide the relevant information. Other sources include abstracts to locate relevant journal articles and personal contact with likely specialists.

Science tends to follow fashion and so scientists are interested to orientate their proposed or actual research within the current scientific value system. Orientation is achieved by a critical reading of recent publications, particularly conference proceedings, with a view to answering questions such as 'why has this topic become popular in preference to other topics in the same area?' and 'which way is the bandwaggon rolling?'. This is particularly necessary at the outset of a project when applications for research funds are being made because unfashionable ideas may be rejected. On the other hand, many interesting and fruitful ideas are not pursued when they drop out of fashion. For example, the early industrial psychology of fatigue represented by the Industrial Health Research Board studies was not developed for several years following the Hawthorne findings of the relevance of social factors in output, only to be revived in a sophisticated form with the emergence of ergonomics in the early 1940's. The scientist who takes note of these changes in fashion, and who does not need large funds, could hit upon a valuable individual line of enquiry.

Information can rarely be taken at its face value, and one of the tasks facing a scientist is to check the reliability of his information and of its sources. Checking may be done by a repetition of experiments or by consulting other independent sources of information. A mere balancing of the quantity of evidence is not sufficient, however, as the odd man out may sometimes be correct. For example, in a situation where three sources give one answer which is contradicted by a fourth source, the three may be derived from one basic (and potentially unreliable) source, whereas the fourth determined the facts afresh. Such a situation can occur when scientists rely on secondary citations and abstracts and fail to check primary sources.

Only the reception of information by the scientist has so far been considered. The creation and transmission of information must also be examined since the main requirements of scientific work are to add new material to the store of accumulated knowledge and to communicate new findings to other scientists. A scientist may publish for reasons of personal security or to increase his status. (The 'publish or perish' philosophy in academic life may be one cause of the so-called 'information explosion'.) Dissemination of information is functional in other ways for a scientist, as well as for science in general. Some forms of communication, particularly the oral presentation at conferences, elicit reactions from other scientists. Questions, additional problems, and indications of defects will help the researcher to see further aspects of his topic. The efforts of the originator are also stimulated and motivated by the act of communication, or even by the anticipation of it. Even social conversation on scientific topics with a ' naive ' layman has a value in that explaining it in simple non-technical language may indicate defects in sequences of argument not previously apparent.

All information must originate from individuals, but two major routes of flow may be considered. The first is direct from one individual to another, by word of mouth, telephone, letter or other personal communication. The communicating individual may be a local colleague or be at a distance in another organisation. The second route is that mediated by published literature. Studies have shown that when a scientist requires information he typically turns to those sources which are most convenient—usually his colleagues in the same laboratory or department, or books in his own bookcase, before using more distant sources such as experts in another department or another organisation or books in a library. This method may not be the most efficient, and ideally the type of information being sought should influence the channel used. For example, when seeking minor procedural details for everyday reference it would be a saving in time and effort to ask a colleague, since this kind of information is rarely recorded in sufficient detail in the literature. When extensive details of conceptual or empirical information are wanted, however, the published literature will prove the better source.

Scientific research should both begin and end in a library. At the outset a comprehensive search is essential both to gain an insight into the area of enquiry and to avoid the wasteful duplication which results from being unaware of the work of others. Not all duplication of research is wasteful, of course, as replication of findings is necessary to check the status of results. Research is wasteful if conducted in ignorance of previous work and with consequent variations in procedure which do not constitute replication. There are, however, differences of opinion as to the value of the initial search. Some authorities consider that reading before action may blunt new ideas and make one follow the set mould of precedent. These views are discussed by Beveridge in *The art of scientific investigation*. He concludes that '. . . in subjects in which knowledge is still growing, or where the particular problem is a new one, or a new version of one already solved, all the advantage is with the expert, but where knowledge is no longer growing and the field has been worked out, a revolutionary new approach is required and this is more likely to come from the outsider ' (page 3).

The extent of preliminary searching seems to depend upon the research worker's personality and objectives. Even the highly original innovator will need minimal information about previous research, if only to indicate where innovation is required, whereas the more mundane plodder will seek much more detailed information. Ignorance may result in wasted effort, but material gained by the initial search must be evaluated critically, as uncritical acceptance of information will extinguish any creative spark. A scientist has not discharged his duty to science and to any financing organisation until his results and findings are communicated in such a way as to assist in further development of his subject.

A critical approach is needed for success both in empirical and literature research. An orderly sequence of operations must be followed with sufficient record made so as to retrace the steps later, as well as to enable another researcher to discern the sequence followed. Persistence and thoroughness are needed especially when few citations and little of interest is being found. Above all, some leavening of imagination must be present to direct the operation in the absence of any logical reason for so proceeding.

CHAPTER 4

DOCUMENTARY AIDS

Using the right tool for the job is a sign of a competent worker. The documentary aids outlined in this chapter are the essential tools for efficient information retrieval, and the research worker will find it worthwhile to familiarise himself with the scope of these tools and to practice their use. The purpose of any documentary aid is to help the researcher discover information quickly and efficiently. Aids may be categorised as primary, secondary or tertiary on the basis of their distance from the original source material (*see* figure 4). Primary source material may be conceptual, empirical or procedural information printed in books, monographs and periodicals, or disseminated by film, tape and other record; or obtained directly from individuals and societies. It may also be material in a physical sense such as drugs, apparatus, etc. Secondary tools do not convey new and original information but list and classify the sources of such information, and so guide the user to primary material. Tertiary tools are once further removed from the original, being lists of secondary tools.

Any item such as a book or periodical may perform more than one function. A book in which the author introduces new concepts is a primary source, but these new concepts may be supported by extensive citations from the literature of the subject, and so this section is a secondary source. Similarly a journal is a vehicle for new information, but it may also contain book reviews and abstracts of papers in other journals (*eg Ergonomics*). Furthermore, the scientist may use tools in ways not recommended by a librarian. For example, because of the delay between primary publication and material appearing in abstract journals, the latter are mainly intended for retrospective searching through the literature. Many scientists use abstracting journals for current awareness purposes, however, and this has put pressure on the compilers to reduce the time lag.

PERIODICALS
Any publication issued in successive parts intended to be published periodically and with no predetermined terminal date is included under

FIGURE 4 : Categorisation of documentary aids

PRIMARY	SECONDARY	TERTIARY
Books	◀ National Bibliography	
Periodicals		
Journals Magazines Newspapers House journals Newsletters		
	Subject bibliography*	◀ Bibliography of bibliographies
	Abstract*	
Reports	Index*	
Government and official publications	Review/digest*	
	Catalogue*	Guide*
	Handbook*	
Standards	Encyclopedia/dictionary*	
Theses	Information service/* clearing house	
Statistics	◀ Guide to sources	
Data	◀ Data bank	
Films		
Organisations	◀ { Conference proceedings	◀ Index to conference proceedings
Individual people	◀ { Directory } { Calendar }	◀ Directory of directories

NB Arrows indicate the most usual coverage.
    Sources starred are likely to cover all or most of the more primary
services.

this heading. Periodicals are essential reading for the specialist as they provide the most up to date information about rapidly developing frontiers of knowledge. New ideas, methods, and data become part of the currency of science following their initial appearance in journal papers. Secondary periodicals such as indexes, abstracts, reviews and bibliographies assist in the process of dissemination by alerting the potential user to information otherwise likely to be missed in the rising flood of literature.

Journals
These take many forms but their major function is as primary sources of information. Some, such as *Science, Nature, Endeavour,* cover the whole of science and help the specialist to keep up to date with areas other than his major specialism. This is of particular value in that concepts and procedures from one branch of science are often found later to influence other branches (for example, information theory developed for telephone engineering is now widely used in psychology). Preliminary announcements of scientific findings are also published in some general science journals (*eg* letters to *Nature*). This information is so important for current awareness that a new class of journal has emerged solely for quick publication of preliminary findings *eg Psychonomic science.*

For any scientist the specialist journals in his subject and related areas may be divided into those of core and peripheral interest. Some of the more common journals of psychology are listed in appendix B. It is impossible for an individual to read all the journals dealing with psychology, but the specialist can decide which journals are likely to carry papers of special interest to him, and which are to be regarded as background reading. Journals differ in the type of information published; some, like *Psychological bulletin* review major areas, others, like *Psychological review* discuss methodological matters, and others, like the *Bulletin of the British Psychological Society* and *American psychologist* are the official organs of psychological organisations and carry news bulletins and information on professional matters. Details of the circulation figures of journals covering psychology were given in the *International journal of psychology,* 1969 *4,* pages 247-250. Most journals publish an annual index to the material included, but it should be noted that these indexes may exclude brief items of news, minor correspondence, notes on books, notes for the guidance of contributors, advertisements and similar information often printed on the covers. This peripheral matter may also be destroyed when single issues are bound. Monographs and monograph supplements are occasionally published with journals to allow a deeper treatment of the subject than could be accommodated within the restrictions of the usual journal paper.

Some current awareness journals consist of the contents page collected from a range of other journals, and thus the scientist is able to scan a wider range of publications than would be available in most libraries. As the contents pages may be received when the primary journal is at a page proof stage, the current awareness journal may also provide the first indication of the publication of a paper. In addition to *Current contents: behavioral, social and management sciences* specialists may find *Current contents: life sciences, Current contents: engineering and technology* and *ABC POL SCI* (Advance bibliography of contents: political science and government) useful. Some organisations and special libraries publish current awareness periodicals which list the material received (*eg* University of Wales Institute of Science and Technology *Current awareness bulletin: occupational psychology*).

Many university departments of psychology publish journals which primarily serve as a training ground for student research publication, and also help to maintain corporate identity. These publications are often irregular, and commence and cease publication with such frequency that it is difficult to keep track of them. Any information of permanent value is most likely to be subsequently published elsewhere, but if reference to one of these publications is essential, often the only way of locating a copy is to ask the relevant department.

House journals and trade literature produced by industrial, commercial and public service organisations for circulation to staff and customers may contain useful information. For example, *SK and F reporter* has articles on social psychiatry and occasional reviews on topics in psychology, *eg* a bibliography of creativity, while the publications of instrument companies suggest uses for their equipment relevant to experimental psychology (*Dawe digest, AIM technical interface, Farnell news* and others). Details of such publications may be found in the annual *Newspaper press directory* and the *Directory of members* of the British Association of Industrial Editors. The contents of some house journals are indexed, for example, *British humanities index* and *British technology index,* and abstracted, *eg Engineering abstracts.*

Many periodical publications variously known as ' newsletters ', ' bulletins ' or ' fact sheets ', exist primarily to convey news, such as forthcoming events, reports of recent events, elections, reports of committees, government activity, about a narrowly circumscribed subject. It is not easy to draw a line between these and the journals which function as official organs of societies in addition to carrying more scholarly articles. The former are frequently small, often duplicated, dependent upon enthusiasm of a small group of people with relatively limited circulation and with a regrettable tendency to cease publication. Details of some newsletters and house journals are given in appendix D.

The current awareness function of newspapers and magazines should not be overlooked, as the first indication of a research project may be a popular article, prepared before the researcher is willing to commit himself to the more rigorous presentation in journals. They may also be a source of raw material for the social psychologist, for example, using content analysis to indicate changes in attitudes, or the industrial psychologist seeking background information about a firm, or industry, or changes in the economy which may influence worker behaviour. Indexes exist to single sources, such as the *Index to the times* and to a group of sources, such as *Readers guide to periodical literature* and *British humanities index.*

Reviews

Reviews of progress in specific areas of a subject are invaluable at the start of a research project, both to set the scene and to provide items for a bibliography. Reviews also help the specialist keep up to date with topics outside his specialism. *Psychological bulletin* and *Annual review of psychology* are probably the most important to psychologists, but other specialised series may also be of considerable value, *eg Advances in child development and behaviour, Progress in brain research.* Some periodical reviews are listed in appendix F. In addition to reviews in periodical form, individual books comprising scholarly reviews can also frequently be found, for example Vroom *Work and motivation.*

Book reviews vary from a simple listing of the contents to a full evaluation of the intellectual contribution of the book when viewed against the present state of knowledge. The former merely supplement the title but are of use in deciding whether to examine the book. The latter function as general reviews of the state of knowledge and make valuable preliminary reading prior to a comprehensive search. It is desirable to consult several reviews of a book, particularly those in interdisciplinary areas to evaluate it from various viewpoints. *Contemporary psychology* and *Psychiatry and social science review* consist entirely of reviews of books and audio-visual aids. *Mental health book review index* (annually) gives bibliographic details and references to a wide variety of books which receive three or more reviews, at least one of which must have been published in a core psychological journal. In this way only those books are included which have created an impact upon several reviewers. *Technical book review index* gives brief extracts and original sources of book reviews but is of limited use in psychology, although it covers mathematical and statistical books.

Indexes

Most periodicals contain an index to each volume, but in addition some secondary periodicals exist solely to index the contents of other publications. Just as the index in a book enables one to find information without checking every page, these indexes to periodicals provide a classified list to the contents of a number of periodicals. *Psychological index* (the forerunner to *Psychological abstracts*) will now be of use only to the historian, but psychologists working in applied areas or at the boundaries between psychology and other disciplines may need to refer to indexes such as *Social sciences and humanities index, Applied science and technology index, Business periodicals index* and *Education index* (*see* figure 5). Some indexes are listed in appendix E. Popular magazines are covered by the *Readers' guide to periodical literature*, pamphlets and other ephemeral materials may be located through the *Vertical file index*, and indexes exist to non-literary materials such as drugs (*Unlisted drugs*), educational visual aids (*Abstracts of instructional materials in technical and vocational education*), films (*British national film catalogue*) and computer programs (*National computer program index*).

It is quicker to refer to these indexes than to leaf through the pages of periodicals, but the efficiency of retrieval by this means will depend upon the comprehensiveness of the index, *ie* the number of primary sources covered and whether the coverage of each is complete or merely selective. The accuracy with which article titles reflect their contents will also influence the efficiency of retrieval. It may be annoying to check a potentially valuable article from an index only to find it completely worthless; it may be tragic to miss an article because its snappy title does not truly indicate its content.

The use of computers has led to a new layout of some indexes known as the ' Keyword ' format. This is produced by the computer scanning titles and collecting together all those with a word in common (obvious common words are ignored) and thus each article will be listed several times according to the number of keywords in the title. A Keyword-in-context (KWIC) index is illustrated in figure 6. It can be seen that very long titles may be truncated depending upon the line output from the computer, but sufficient will remain to identify material of interest. The keyword approach makes it easier to find information, but underlines the importance of an adequate title. A human indexer may note that a paper entitled 'All the red legged partridges ' is about scientific information techniques, but computers are not yet sufficiently intelligent. Some services use subject specialists to supplement titles by adding relevant words. For example, the *Biological abstracts* KWIC index adds information to identify the type of investigation, the type of article, techniques and locality.

A citation index is based on the principle that authors cite previous studies upon which their work is based. *Science citation index* covers a large number of journals (over 2,000 in 1969, of which ninety were psychology journals) and uses a computer to list together details of documents in which a common reference is cited. Figure 7 is an extract from *Science citation index* which shows that Broadbent's paper (in *British journal of psychology* 1953, *44,* page 295) was cited by Boggs (in *Journal of applied psychology* 1968, *52,* page 148), and that *Perception and communication* was cited thirteen times. The titles of citing papers are given in the source index, and the organisation index indicates organisations where the published research was undertaken. The method of using *SCI* is different from most other indexing systems in that the search starts from a specific citation rather than from a subject heading. This citation may have been found in previous searches or in handbooks and similar publications. The basic question asked is ' where and by whom has this work been cited in the litera-

39

FIGURE 5: An extract from *Education index*

Attitudinal outcomes of eight-week Head start teacher-training programs with the Parental attitude research instrument. M. E. Burrett. Childh Ed 46:115-17 N '69
Creative supervision of Head start centers. V. B. Hatch. Young Children 25:96-101 D '69
Evaluation of Head start programs; NCTE/ERIC report. R. V. Denby. El Engl 46:1053-62 D '69

Follow through programs

Morgan follows through. S. Moorefield. il Am Ed 6:31-3 Ja '70

PROJECT re-ed. See Emotionally disturbed children—Education

PROJECT talent test battery
Development of moderated scoring keys for psychological inventories: Student information blank. D. J. Prediger. bibliog Ed & Psychol M 29:813-24 Wint '69
Jensen's theory of intelligence; with reply by A. R. Jensen and rejoinder. L. G. Humphreys and H. P. Dachler. bibliog J Ed Psychol 60:419-33 D '69

PROJECTILES
See also
Rockets

PROJECTION
See also
Map projection

PROJECTION apparatus
Aids we should never have had to do without. D. J. Reid. Times Ed Sup 2841:33 O 31 '69
Mini drawing instruments yield maxi results. G. C. Stegemiller. il Sch Shop 29:51 Ja '70
New look filmstrip projectors. N. Willis. il Times Ed Sup 2837:41 O 3 '69
Overhead projection revelation techniques. M. W. Seng. il Ed Screen AV G 48:12-13 D '69
Projection pointers. F. S. Lestingi. See issues of Physics teacher
Visumodule approach to overhead projection. F. K. Utley. il AV Instr 15:80-1 Ja '70

PROJECTION rooms
SUNY learning resources focus on multimedia lecture rooms. il Col & Univ Bsns 48:68 Ja '70

PROJECTIVE tests
See also
Vineland ego development profile

PROJECTS

Second grades

Yes, we play post office! C. Bown. il Grade Teach 87:76-7 Ja '70

PROPAGANDA
See also
Radio broadcasting—Propaganda

PROPORTION. See Ratio and proportion

PROTEINS
Student experiments on the gel filtration of proteins. F. Dewhurst. J Chem Ed 46:864-5 D '69

PRUDDEN, Bonnie
Challenge, change, rhythm. J. D. Havlick. J Phys Ed 67:36-7 N '69

PRUKOP, Al
Study guide for off-season instruction of quarterbacks. Athletic J 50:48+ Ja '70

PRYOR, Marvin J.
Stir about convection currents. Phys Teach 7:398 O '69

PSYCHOLOGICAL measurement. See Psychometrics

PSYCHOLOGICAL research

Methodology

Disproportionality of cell frequencies in psychological and educational experiments involving multiple classification. R. K. Steinhorst and C. D. Miller. bibliog Ed & Psychol M 29:799-811 Wint '69

PSYCHOLOGISTS
See also
Burt, C. L.
Rogers, C. R.

PSYCHOLOGY
See also
Association (psychology)
Dissonance (psychology)
Fantasy
Perception
Symbolization
Transposition (psychology)

PSYCHOLOGY, Educational

Achievements, Student

Study of evaluation in social science oriented educational psychology courses; Redwood school test. J. W. Johnson and R. S. Waldrop. Ed & Psychol M 29:969-76 Wint '69

Tests and scales

Study of evaluation in social science oriented educational psychology courses; Redwood school test. J. W. Johnson and R. S. Waldrop. Ed & Psychol M 29:969-76 Wint '69

PSYCHOLOGY, Industrial
Correlates of employee evaluations of pay increases. J. R. Hinrichs. bibliog J Ap Psychol 53:481-9 D '69
Effects of performance on leadership, cohesiveness, influence, satisfaction, and subsequent performance. G. F. Farris and F. G. Lim, jr. bibliog J Ap Psychol 53:490-7 D '69

PSYCHOLOGY, Pathological
See also
Hypochondria

PSYCHOLOGY, Physiological
Cardio-vascular and respiratory changes accompanying hypnotic physical stress R. Jirka. J Phys Ed 67:51-2 N '69
Effect of hostility on physiological and fantasy responses. A. M. Barclay. bibliog J Personal 37:651-67 D '69.
Role of arousal and cognitive complexity in susceptibility to social influence. V. K. Corfield. bibliog J Personal 37:554-66 D '69
See also
Drugs—Psychological effect

PSYCHOMETRICS

Research

Establishment of a National research institute for the construction and standardization of tests. A. Bannatyne. J Learn Dis 2:659-60 D '69

PSYCHOTHERAPY

Group work

Talking group therapy for learning-disabled children. L. Wright and C. McKenzie. Read Teach 23:339-46 Ja '70
Use of group processes in teaching retarded readers. R. R. Edelstein. Read Teach 23:318-24 Ja '70

PUBLIC health

Egypt

Prevalence and causes of blindness in a developing country: a preliminary report. M. E. Said and others. Sight-Saving R 39:158-61 Fall '69

PUBLIC institutions

Employees

Georgia

Ward language development program for institutionalized retardates; attendants attempt to stimulate the ward environment of the children. F. W. Bennett. Train Sch Bul 66:23-31 My '69

PUBLIC relations
In-service education: Marshall community unit schools. D. Shawler and R. Griffiths. Ill Ed 58:150-1 D '69
Public relations. C. H. Harrison. See issues of Nation's schools January 1970-
Public relations pay. B. J. Ball. Sch & Com 56:14 Ja '70
Schoolmen aren't bragging about their PR programs; school administrators opinion poll. Nations Sch 85:31 Ja '70
See also
Libraries—Public relations

Adult schools and classes

Pathways to public favor in adult education. K. Baugrud. Adult Lead 18:177-8+ D '69

PUBLIC relations directors
This board member casts his vote for a district public relations man. H. W. Hoover. Am Sch Bd J 157:34 Ja '70

PUBLIC schools

Criticism

Carl Rogers joins ranks of radical critics of the public schools. Phi Delta Kappan 51:294 Ja '70 ture?'. In addition a guide is available which suggests many uses for *SCI*. Some of the more obvious are to check whether a hint for further research has been followed, a new method used, or a book reviewed. A very useful function is to assist in bringing subject bibliographies up to date. It is necessary to enter the system with older material, however, because of the inevitable time lag before very recent articles become sufficiently well known to receive extensive citations.

Abstracts

Whereas indexes merely list articles, abstracts additionally give brief summaries of the essential points of published papers, books, etc, and thus the reader is able to decide whether the original is likely to be of interest. *Psychological abstracts* (*see* figure 8) is probably the most widely used single bibliographical tool in psychology. The delay between original publication of an article and the publication of its summary in *Psychological abstracts* is now sufficiently short for it to be used as a current awareness device, and its coverage of psychology is so wide that it is generally the first choice when compiling a bibliography by retrospective searching. Psychology is envied by many other sciences which do not possess such an extensive system, but the psychologist should be aware that other abstracting systems exist and that some of these may be of use. Because of the extensive scattering of psychological literature, *Psychological abstracts* cannot be expected to contain everything likely to be of interest to all psychologists. Daniel (' Psychology ' *Library trends* 1967, 15 4, 670-684) stated that at best, it could be expected to supply eighty five percent of required references and quoted evidence that this percentage would be much lower for foreign language and interdisciplinary material. *Biological abstracts* have a sharing system whereby some interesting abstracts from *Biological abstracts* are published in *Psychological abstracts* and vice versa; but the psychologist working on the physiological and animal behaviour fringes of psychology would probably benefit by checking the appropriate sections in *Biological abstracts*. Similarly, psychologists might use *Child development abstracts, Training abstracts, Excerpta medica,* etc. A list of abstracts is given in appendix E. Considerable overlap exists between abstracting services, but it is better to have several leads to an important document than to risk missing it. Furthermore, the same original article can appear in a very different

41

2*

FIGURE 6: Keyword-in-Context index (from *Perceptual cognitive development*)

```
ck* Adaptation to prismatically    displaced vision as a function of degree of displacement and amount of feedba   VAN E -AR-4551
ed vision as a function of degree of   displacement and amount of feedback* Adaptation to prismatically displac    VAM E -AR-4551
the relation of adaptation to field    displacement during head movements to the constancy of visual direction* On   WALLH -AR-5391
                      Perceptual       displacement of a test mark toward the larger of two visual objects*           MPRCT-AR-0155
             * Effects of altered      display-control relationships on information processing from a visual display   SIMOJR-AR-4916
             Recording, analyzing, and  displaying spatio-temporal position data*                                     PEDEDM-AR-4582
             processing of tachistoscopic  displays with controlled order of characters and spaces*                    SHAWPD-AR-4770
perception of briefly exposed visual   displays* A multicomponent theory of the                                       RUMEDE-AP-4882
                        On the         disruption of short-term memory by a response prefix*                          IOWEDG-AP-5050
        reported by male subjects*     dissatisfaction and sensation-seeking as related to frequency of daydreaming   WINDG -AR-4570
and learning: The use of drugs for-    dissecting out mechanisms of conditioned behavior* Brain catecholamines        RCCHPR-OR-5428
en personality and performance under   dissimilar modes of instruction* Differential relationships betwe             MAJEK -AP-4526
grasshoppers, cognitive camels, and    dissonance  Philip G. Zimbardo  The cognitive control of motivation. Glenvie  DE CR -BR-0870
d teachers* The effects of cognitive   dissonance on students' cognitive differentiation of positively-valued and ne  SOMCE -AB-4720
cement familiarity and intensity on    dissonance reactions of cognitively naive children* The effect of reinfo       OSTPBM-AB-4742
rst grade children* Use of cognitive   dissonance to produce changes in the attitudes and behavior of economically d  LEONT-AB-5193
               Interpersonal           distance and impression formation*                                            PATTML-AR-5193
               A test of the           distinction between short-term memory and long-term memory*                   GROWLD-AR-4899
                                       Distortion of figural experience and augmented paradoxical sleep*             MEPCD -OP-5422
                                       Distortion of figural compositional information in intermodal transmission*    KUMRIJ-AR-0277
ler protocol sheets* A comparison of   distortion scores on the bender visual motor gestalt test using circular and   WANDWJ-AB-4809
       School-related perceptions in   distortion thresholds in the Ames room* The                                    STLBRM-AB-5039
d and expanded speech by emotionally   distractor task: Initial and second choice performance*                        RUMDD -AP-4888
eception teaching strategies on high   distractors in problem solving*                                                 MAIENR-BP-0331
toward achievement to convergent and   distribution function*                                                         PALMJ -TR-0218
       Short-term incubation in        distribution of practice on retention* Adaptation to                           DEWAR -AR-5005
strategies on high divergent and low   disturbed children*                                                            TMOMBC-AR-4556
ion with cognitive, attitudinal, and   disturbed children* Comprehension of compresse                                 STAPPC-AB-4733
                                       divergent and low divergent thinkers in mathematics* A problem of the effects  ROBIJW-OM-5244
                                       divergent problem-solving* The relationship of orientation                     ELKISH-AB-4619
                                       divergent production*                                                          FULGA -AR-4956
                                       divergent thinkers* A problem of the effects of inductive-guid                 ROBIJW-OM-5244
                                       divergent thinking variables* Achievement prediction in nursing educat         OWENSV-AR-5532
                                       divergent-convergent abilities*                                                UNMSMJ-AR-4255
                Dogmatism and          divine discontent?  Frank Barron  Creative person and creative process.  New Y  STORA -BP-4490
Reviewed in* Creativity measured by    documentary history - Vol 1, 1600-1865*                                        BREMPH-RK-5314
Children and youth in America: A       DOE* Altered free asso                                                          WEINM -AP-4508
ciations: Some cognitive effects of    Dogmatism and college achievement*                                            SEEGJE-AB-4791
                                       Dogmatism and divergent-convergent abilities*                                  UHMSMJ-AP-4255
                                       Dogmatism and divergent-convergent abilities in seminary students*             WIEMMJ-AB-1764
                                       Dogmatism and future time perspective in seminary students*                    AGRKM -AR-4880
                                       Dogmatism and the verbal behavior of student teachers*                         LONGHB-AB-5253

            Information sources,        Dogmatism, and judgmental modifications*
```

FIGURE 7: Extracts from *Science citation index*

Citation Index

```
BROADBEN AD----------------*65 CHEM COMM-----------------107
  BROADBEN-AD----65-TETRAHEDRON LETTERS----------------509
    BROADBEN-AD------J CHEM      R 68--------------------2079
    PIETRZYK DJ----67-ANAL CHEM ACTA-- R 68---------R124
      PIETRZYK DJ----67-ANAL CHEM      R 68-----------3094
BRODABEN-AD------J CHEM S B--------------------------519
  BRODABEN-AD----J CHEM S B-- R 68--------------------R194
  BRDZYK DJ-931*ANGLEY ORTHODONTICS----------------470
MALDEN RH--------31-ANGLE ORTHODONTIS--------------41
PLASR SURG----------------------------------------465
  KOPPL MJ--------AMJ ORTHOD----------------------------565
  PLAT JA----------AMJ ORTHOD----------------------------54
  JUHARA BS--------ANGL ORTHOD--------------------------38
BROADBEN-AD------*66-J CHEM SOC------------------------A
BRDABEN-AD----*53-ORTHESM J PSYCHOLOGY--------------295
BROADBEN RJ 453----J APPL PSYCHOL----------------------146
  BOGGS DH--------54-J APPL PSYCHOL-- 60-----------------67
    XATL P----------NATURE--------------------------------218
    BOGGS DH--------54-QUARP PSYC EXPERIME--------------50
      MURRAY DJ------54-Q J EXP PSYCHOL--------------------58 CH10
      BOGGS DH--------57-HANDBOOK NOISE CONTR----------CH10
BOGGS DH------------J APPL PSYCHOL--------------------52
  BOGGS DH--------57-PSYCHOLOGICAL REVIEW------------207
    HART RO--------57-J ADM PSYCH IN--------------------73
      INGLIS J------57-PSYCH J EXP PSYCHOL--------------27
      * INGLIS J----58-J ACOUSTICAL SOCIETY----------42
        KARLIN L------58-J J PSYCHO------------------------148
BOGGS DH------------58-PLAY HUMAN COMMUN--------------52
  BOGGS DH--------J APPL PSYC--------------------------52
    LUCE RAN------PERKEP PSYCH--------------------------66
    HAKKUM ER----CAN J PSYCH--------------------------23
    MOTT C--------ALT PSYCH--------------------------------28
    INGLIS J------CHEM ENG N--------------------------------68
    KARLEN L------BR J EXP PSY--------------------------167
    MURDOCK BB----BR J PSYCHO--------------------------558
    MURDOCK BB----BR J PSYCHO--------------------------421
    KASPAPUR-M----J ENVIRONMENT----------------------146
    BOGGS DH------61-BEHAVIOUR AU----------------------17
    MORTON HA----BR J PSYCHO--------------------------465
  HAUSIN MC------62-BRIT J J PSYCHOL----------------103
    KRAILC FIM----BRIT J PSYCHO--------------------------58
    TAUB HA--------J GERONTOL--------------------------68
      TAUB HA------ACTA PSYCHOLOGICA----------------122
    FUSHMER RF----63-SCIENCE----------------------------204
  BROADBEN-DE----63-BR J PSYCHOL----------------------300
    KRITAUCIU-R----CURREC LEARN VERB BE--------------34
    MURDOCK BB----J GERONTOL--------------------------169
    MURDOCK BB----BR J PSYCHO--------------------------421
      MURDOCK BB----J EXP PSYCH--------------------------68
    BOGGS DH------64-ACTA PSYCHOLOGICA----------------52
BROADBEN-DE----64-DISORDERS LANGUAGE C-----------77
ANISFELD M------J EXP PSYCH------------------------171
KRYTER KD------AM PSYCHOL--------------------------262
```

Source Index

```
BOGE S
  ARCH MATH    19  125 68      5R N2  03673
    ALGEBRAIC DEMONSTRATION OF A THEOREM OF RITT
    FROM ALGEBRAIC DIFFERENTIAL EQUATION THEORY
BOGEN PM
      SUGITA KH    WITULSKI M    RUSBULDT D
      NOLL         WAELBROE F
  PLASMA PHYS 10  437 68 M  NO  NA  A8306
    RECENT RESULTS FROM JULICH THETA PINCH
    EXPERIMENTS
BOGENSCH-AF KRAHL  PH
  METALL        22  595 68      49R N6  B2235
    METALL-CONTAINING SCREEN PRINTING MIXTURES FOR
    ELECTRONIC CIRCUITS
BOGENSCH-AF SEE SCHWARTZ B  J ELCHEM SO 115  677
BOGGS DH-AF SIMON JR                28R N2  A9487
  J APPL PSYC  52  148 68
    DIFFERENTIAL EFFECT OF NOISE ON TASKS OF
    VARYING COMPLEXITY
BOGGS DR  MARSH JC    CHERVENI-PA  CARTWRIG-GE
  P SOC EXP N 127  689 68      7R  N3  B 614
    NEUTROPHIL RELEASING ACTIVITY IN PLASMA OF
    NORMAL HUMAN SUBJECTS INJECTED WITH ENDOTOXIN
BOGGS DR  SEE CHERVENI-PA  J CLIN INV    47 A 19
BOGGS DR  SEE MARSH JC     J PEDIAT      71   15
BOGGS JE  SEE EGAN T       J PEDIAT      72  570
BOGGS JE  SEE MURPHY JS    B AM PHYS S   13  834
BOGGS JE  SEE WANG IYM     J CHEM PHYS   48  812
BOGGS PP  SEE QUINTANA RP  J COLL I SC   26  166
```

43

FIGURE 8: An extract from *Psychological abstracts*

score. *Journal of Applied Psychology*, 1970, **54**(3), 208–210.—Describes 3 relatively simple computer algo-rithms for estimating the average number of sylla-bles/word in text from letter counts. The syllable counts were used to determine Flesch Reading Ease Scores for text by computer. Vowel counts worked well.—*Journal abstract.*

11604. **Kiselëv, A. & Miroshnichenko, L. Primenenie elektronno-vychislitel'noi mashiny v psikhiatrii.** [The application of the electronic computer in psychiatry.] *Zhurnal Nevropatologii i Psikhiatrii*, 1969, **69**(8), 1244–1250.—Presents a survey of the non-Soviet literature. Specific aspects of the electronic computer in psychiatry that are reviewed include: (a) recording, storage, and retrieval of information; (b) analysis of accrued infor-mation; (c) appropriate lexicon; and (d) diagnosis. (64 ref.)—*I. D. London.*

11605. **Miller, R. B.** (IBM, Poughkeepsie, N.Y.) **Archetypes in man-computer problem solving.** *Er-gonomics*, 1969, **12**(4), 559–581.—An analysis of human problem-solving tasks reveals the following: simple inquiry and update, status inquiry, briefing, exception detection, diagnosis, planning/choosing, evaluating/op-timizing, constructing (designing), and discovery. There is no compulsive ordering of these on a complexity scale. The information processing structure of each is exam-ined; some common denominators among this set reveal 5 archetypes of interaction. By making these archetypes explicit and consistent with concepts of domain, application disciplines and system design can move in parallel and generate a simple, well-defined language structure between system and human user.—*Journal abstract.*

clude: (a) user pacing and optional repetition of speech output in a transactional sequence, (b) use of different voices and other auditory coding to distinguish types of output, and (c) use of tone codes to indicate required input.—*Journal abstract.*

TESTING.

11608. **Nowakowska, Maria. Pewne psychologic-zne problemy psychometrii.** [Certain psychological issues of psychometry.] *Przegląd Psychologiczny*, 1969, No. 17, 15–28.—Presented a theoretical analysis of the concept of trait which resulted in a new approach to the axiomatics of the classical test theory. Cattell's (see 39:1 and 36:2) ideas were used to construct a new stronger variant of an axiomatics presupposing some a priori knowledge of the nature of the trait measured. This new variant appeared to provide a bridge between the psychological theories which define given traits and psychometry as the technique of trait measurement. (Russian summary)—*English summary.*

11609. **Strowig, R. Wray & Alexakos, C. E.** (U. Northern Iowa) **Overlap between achievement and aptitude scores.** *Measurement & Evaluation in Gui-dance*, 1969, **2**(3), 157–167.—2 types of factor analysis were used to study 21 measurements, 9 of aptitude, and 12 of achievement. Ss were 122 high school seniors. Results indicate that most aptitude variables could be considered distinct entities, while most achievement variables clustered around a general achievement factor. —*S. M. Amatora.*

light when abstracted from different points of view. One system may stress theory and another stress applications.

Apart from these systems which attempt to cover all the literature in a subject, there are some which cover all the literature published in one language or group of languages, or by a group of countries. The Russian *Referativnyi zhurnal* is published in over fifty sections, but there is not one which specifically includes psychology. Items from *Referativnyi zhurnal (biologiya)* are likely to be found in *Biological abstracts,* and those from *Meditsinskii referativnyi zhurnal* are included in *Excerpta medica.* The *Psychologie* section of the French *Bulletin signaletique* may be of use but is likely only to supplement *Psychological abstracts* in its coverage of European medical and philosophical literature.

Bibliographies

Librarians distinguish many different forms of bibliography, but all are lists of published documents, and three types are important for the scientist. These are national or comprehensive, subject, and bibliographies of bibliography.

A national bibliography attempts to list everything published within that country. Though these are produced in many parts of the world, the *British national bibliography,* American *Cumulative book index, Bibliographie de la France, Deutsche bibliographie* and Russian *Ezhogodnik knigi,* are probably the most useful to the psychologist. Abstracts are included in the monthly *Bulletin critique du livre Français.* The individual editions of national bibliographies are useful for current awareness, and the annual cumulations are classified in detail and so save time when doing a retrospective search. In addition to the official national bibliographies, there are several commercial services particularly intended for the book trade. These may indicate forthcoming books as well as those actually published, *eg* Whitaker's *Books of the month and books to come*—British, and Bowker's *Forthcoming books* —American.

Governments publish large amounts of information and frequently have the largest output of documents in a country, but these documents are often difficult to trace, and so government catalogues are useful. Amongst these are HMSO daily and monthly *List of government publications,* annual *Government publications catalogue,* and the

45

American *Monthly catalog of US government publications* with annual index. Publications of the United Nations and its many specialised agencies such as UNESCO and the World Health Organisation may be traced through *UN documents index*. In addition, there are guides to scientific output of particular countries, such as *Abstracts of Bulgarian scientific literature* and *Japan science review*.

General bibliographies of psychology are provided by the *American behavioral scientist* and the American Bibliographic Service *Quarterly checklist of psychology* covers new nonperiodical material in many Western languages. The new psychological literature of Germany, Austria and Switzerland is listed in *Psychologische rundschau*, and that of Bulgaria, Czechoslovakia, East Germany, Poland, Rumania, Hungary and the USSR in *Bibliographie der psychologischen Literatur aus sozialistischen Ländern vom Jahr . . .* (annually). *Contemporary psychology* carries lists of recent foreign books (Russian, German, Slavic, etc, titles of which are translated into English).

Subject bibliographies attempt to list all the published documents which are relevant to a specific topic. A good bibliography should give the criteria for inclusion of items and the date limits of material considered; the latter is particularly useful when updating an existing bibliography. Annotated bibliographies are particularly useful when they give sufficient information to indicate whether a document is likely to be worth further examination. Many subject bibliographies are included in *Psychological abstracts;* reviews, handbooks, encyclopedias and theses being additional sources. Some subject bibliographies are published in a book form, *eg* Kendall and Doig *Bibliography of statistical literature*. Reading or book lists are sometimes dignified by the title ' bibliography ' but these are usually not sufficiently comprehensive to qualify. This is not to say, though, that they are without value, particularly to introduce a new aspect of a subject. A good example is the *Harvard list of books in psychology*.

A good subject bibliography takes much time and effort to compile, and so it is desirable first to check whether one already exists. Some useful bibliographies of bibliographies are *Bibliographic index*, ASTIA *Bibliography of bibliographies* and Besterman *A world bibliography of bibliographies*. The Bibliography of Soviet bibliographies (*Bibliografiva sovietkoi bibliografii*) lists bibliographies which contain more than thirty items appearing in Soviet journals. Similar compilations are available for bibliographies in German (*Bibliographie der deutschen Bibliographien*) and French (*Bulletin de documentation bibliographique* and *Repertoire annuel des principaux travaux bibliographiques recents*).

BOOKS

It is important to distinguish between the two uses of the word ' book '. One use concerns the format of the item, which may contain anything from a catalogue of a great library, such as the *London bibliography of the social sciences*, to the cumulation of an index, such as *Cumulated subject index to psychological abstracts*. The more important use in the present context concerns the content; whether primary, secondary or tertiary. It is not possible in the limits of a work such as this to discuss books as primary source material, since this would be an extensive undertaking which would quickly be out of date. Secondary and tertiary books include handbooks (whether or not this is included in the title), textbooks, dictionaries, encyclopedias, yearbooks, directories and biographical guides. Titles are notoriously misleading, as a ' yearbook ' may not appear annually (*eg* Buros' *Mental measurements yearbook*), and a ' dictionary ' may be sufficiently comprehensive to be termed an ' encyclopedia ' (*eg* Baldwin *Dictionary of philosophy and psychology*). In seeking books, the searcher should remember that some long-established and frequently revised works are still referred to by their original author's name, *eg* Gray's *Anatomy of the human body* edited by Goss, C M. In a rapidly developing area, books may be more or less out of date when they are published and so it is important to check the date of writing (suggested ways of evaluating books are given in chapter 8). A wide variety of books can be identified through bibliographies.

Handbooks

The aim of a handbook is systematically to collate and digest facts and methods scattered through the periodical literature. They are mainly of use as everyday reference tools, but they may also serve as textbooks for advanced students and help to fill in the background to a topic at the outset of a research project. Some of the more common handbooks in psychology and related subjects are listed in appendix G.

47

Textbooks

Textbooks are basically intended as teaching aids, but those concerned with advanced material and specialised areas may be used as handbooks, eg Hays *Statistics for psychologists*. Textbooks in related fields may be useful to give an overall picture of the field to psychologists who do not require a detailed understanding. A recent development in textbook publishing has been the introduction of series of elementary monographs, each one dealing with a specific area, and thus able to cover in more detail the material which would be included in one chapter of the omnibus textbook, eg Prentice-Hall *Foundations of modern psychology*. *Contemporary psychology* frequently contains reviews which compare and evaluate the available textbooks, both at the introductory level and the various specialisms within psychology.

Textbooks in programmed format are being published in increasing numbers, but their advantage as pedagogic instruments must be weighed against their drawback for quick reference. All kinds of programmed instructional material (such as books, teaching machines, films) are included in a list of ' Programmes in Print ' in the *Yearbook of educational and instructional technology*. This list is kept up to date with quarterly supplements in the journal *Programmed learning and educational technology*, and news of developments in this area is given in ' Programmed Learning News ', monthly in *Visual education*.

Collections of readings

Extracts from important scientific papers are published as collections of readings to supplement the material in elementary textbooks. These are useful in providing details of the background and highlighting the development of specialised areas, and they may also include extensive lists of references which could be used in the preparation of research bibliographies. Similar functions are served by collected papers of outstanding researchers republished in book form eg Stouffer, *Social research to test ideas* and ' festschriften ', eg Banks and Broadburst, *Stephanos: studies in psychology*). ' Readings ' should not be confused with reports of symposia and conferences, where new information and work in progress may be recorded (*see* page 54). The confusion over titles is particularly unfortunate in this respect and the user must check the nature of the document by careful reading of preface, introduction, etc.

Yearbooks

Three uses of this term may be distinguished:

(i) as a directory, such as *Industrial training yearbook;*

(ii) as a handbook, such as Buros' *Mental measurements yearbook;*

(iii) as an annual review, such as *Yearbook of neurology and neurosurgery.*

For details see the appropriate sections of this chapter.

Encyclopedias

These are comprehensive works presenting the state of knowledge at a given time. They may be universal, *eg Britannica, Chambers* or limited to a single subject or group of subjects, *eg International encyclopaedia of social sciences.* Advanced students and research workers often do not consider encyclopedias as documentary aids, but a good general encyclopedia may be a useful starting point for general orientation at the beginning of a project. Specialised encyclopedias can also be of use in this way, as well as functioning as handbooks for everyday reference. One drawback is that because of their size, encyclopedias are not revised very frequently and so articles on rapidly developing aspects of science soon become out of date. Some specialised encyclopedias are listed with handbooks in appendix G.

Dictionaries

There is no clear dividing line between dictionaries and encyclopedias, although the former mainly consider words as linguistic entities, and the latter consider the ideas and objects which the words represent. Several types of dictionaries are useful. In scientific reporting it is essential to find words which exactly express a concept and so a thesaurus is useful to supply synonyms which vary in fine shades of meaning. The precise meaning of words will be found in a general English language dictionary, but recent technical and scientific words are unlikely to be found here and so a technical and scientific dictionary will be necessary. Psychologists have coined many new terms, and may use existing words in different ways, and so the meaning of these should be checked in a dictionary of psychology. (For example, English, H C and English A C *A comprehensive dictionary of psychological and psychoanalytical terms* gives six different specialised uses of ' set '.) Specialised dictionaries in related areas such as psychiatry, zoology and electronics may also be necessary. English language dictionaries of psychology and related subjects are given in appendix I.

A general translating dictionary (bi-lingual or multi-lingual) is necessary when reading foreign material. Specialised, scientific and technical words may not be included in this, and so a technical translating dictionary with sufficient psychological terms will be necessary. The scientist with some familiarity of a foreign language will find mono-lingual foreign language dictionaries and mono-lingual scientific and technical dictionaries useful for checking exact nuances of meaning in the original text. Sources of foreign language scientific dictionaries together with some foreign language dictionaries of psychology are given in appendix H.

Directories

These are of obvious use for tracking down individuals and societies, institutions and similar organisations, some of which are mentioned in chapter I under ' Psychological Research '. Individual psychologists may be located through the membership lists of the various national psychological societies, such as the annual British Psychological Society *List of members,* and the American Psychological Association *Directory.* Duijker, H C J and Jacobson, E H *International directory of psychologists* (second edition), Royal Van Gorcum, 1966 is now out of date, but a third edition is in preparation.

Directories of research in progress are invaluable for locating individuals with specialised knowledge or for checking whether a proposed research topic has already been investigated, *eg Register of research into higher education, Scientific research in British universities and colleges*—kept up to date by the *SSRC newsletter.* Directories of foundations may help to locate funds for a project, *eg* the British National Council of Social Service's *Directory of grant making trusts,* Giovanni Agnetti Foundation's *Directory of European foundations,* and the American Foundation Library Center's *Foundation directory.* For eminent individuals, biographical information such as specialisation, career history, publications and present position may be recorded in biographical directories, *eg American men of science, Directory of British scientists.* Apart from its uses for biographical journalism, such information can be very useful in compiling a subject bibliography. The merest clue may yield extensive information. For example, the possession of an honorary degree will indicate that a university may have published a citation of his outstanding achievements, and BPS and APA prize winners will be similarly recognised. Some journals publish biographical information about contributors. *Who's who* or a biographical dictionary may indicate date of death of notable scholars, and an obituary published in a professional journal may provide an extensive bibliography.

In view of the quantity and variety of available directories, the use of a directory of directories is recommended (*see Current British directories, Current European directories, Guide to American directories*).

Theses and dissertations
These are useful sources of information as they generally contain a scholarly review of the relevant literature. Original findings are subsequently published in the appropriate journals, but a thesis will still have value in yielding full details of methods and procedures used together with more extensive data. *Dissertation abstracts international* is not as extensive as its title would indicate, and until recently it only covered US and Canadian universities. 'International' was added to the title in the expectation of including European theses in the future. The publishers have arrangements with many universities to microfilm doctoral dissertations, but not all universities co-operate nor are all dissertations presented in the co-operating universities included. *Doctoral dissertations accepted by American universities* is an attempt to index all titles accepted by American and Canadian universities, whilst the British equivalent also includes masters' theses (ASLIB *Index to theses accepted for higher degrees in universities of Great Britain and Ireland*). Unfortunately though, there is considerable delay between thesis publication and indexing. Some European national bibliographies include theses. Information about a thesis may be given in a review before details are given in other sources, since specialist reviewers are likely to be aware of work in progress and material recently presented through their network of personal contacts.

Reports
Theses can be as detailed or as concise as required to cover their topic, since they generally do not have to satisfy commercial and financial considerations. Annual reports of organisations which conduct or spon-

sor research are very useful for research intelligence purposes by revealing details of research in progress, the trend of scientific development over a period, and the type of investigation sponsored by the organisation. The latter information could be very useful when making application for research funds. Reports of investigations of all kinds are prepared for organisations which include government departments (*eg* Medical Research Council), international organisations (*eg* OECD, ILO), industrial and commercial organisations, universities, trusts and foundations (*eg* Ciba, Nuffield). Reports may be published by, and catalogued under, the name of the organisation and may also be distinguished from ordinary books by their serial numbers (normally a combination of letters and numbers). Nevertheless many reports do not receive a wide circulation and are difficult to obtain. Some useful aids are the *NLL announcements bulletin, Index to US government research and development reports,* and *Scientific and technical aerospace reports* (this is more general than its name implies, and covers psychology both as ' bioscience ' and ' biotechnology '). *Research in education* covers both projects in progress and completed research and microfiche copies of the latter are available from the National Lending Library. A section in *Nature* lists ' Reports and other publications ' but unfortunately these are not classified by subject but simply divided into British and foreign.

Guides

Comprehensive guides to all types of documentation, and guides to specific subjects related to psychology are given in appendix J.

MISCELLANEOUS OTHER AIDS

Meetings: From a scientific point of view meetings can be divided into two categories by a consideration of the participants. The more frequent occurrences are known variously as congresses, conventions and conferences. At these all who qualify by reason of membership of an appropriate society may attend to read or hear papers and participate in discussions. Direct participation in symposia, colloquia, etc is however limited to a select few experts.

Six important aspects of a conference may be distinguished from a bibliographic point of view. The preliminary announcement indicates the type of papers to be presented (the subject matter of the meeting) and may ask intending speakers to submit abstracts. Meetings organised by psychological organisations are announced in the appropriate official organs, and details of forthcoming meetings will be found in *Scientific meetings*, *Technical meeting index*, and the *Annual international congress calendar*. Conference programmes, which list the papers to be given and details of the qualifications and employing agency of participants, may be useful for research intelligence (orientation). Some institutions and individuals are acknowledged to be in the forefront of scientific advance, and trends in future development may be predicted from their presentations. Time is at a premium in a conference with more intending speakers than programmable space and there is a limit to the amount of information which can be disseminated in the short time available. Some organisations circulate preprint papers to all participants, or to all who ask for particular papers, as one solution to this problem. The whole of the speaker's time can then be devoted to questions and discussion. Preprints* should not be confused with abstracts. The latter are simply summaries (about 200-400 words) which attempt to summarise the kind of information to be given in papers so that participants can decide which to hear. These are potentially unreliable sources of information frequently composed some months before the actual conference and intended to impress the committee responsible for selecting papers. Thus they often contain what the author hopes to be able to present and the actual papers may be far more modest and consequently not published elsewhere.

Information exchanged during the meeting itself is not limited to factual accounts of ideas, methods and results. One advantage of presenting a paper is that it identifies the speaker as being interested in a topic, and as a result may become the focal point of a lively discussion after the formal session. Many scientists report that these discussions are the most valuable part of conferences. Post-conference proceedings published in book or report form provide up to date reviews. A particular difficulty is that proceedings of international conferences are frequently published in a different form by a different publisher following each conference. Details of the published proceedings of International Congresses of Psychology are given in Foss, B M (*ed*) *Psychology in Great Britain*: a supplement to the *Bulletin of the British*

* Also sometimes known as ' Proceedings ' (*eg* Proceedings of the . . . annual convention of the American Psychological Association).

Psychological Society 1969. The *Directory of published proceedings* and the monthly *Index of conference proceedings received by the NLL* may be useful for tracing published proceedings and the *World list of scientific periodicals* (fourth edition) gives a list of periodic international conferences.

SYMPOSIA

Regular congregations of advanced research workers for the purpose of discussing research is a typically American phenomenon, *eg* Nebraska symposium on motivation, Phi delta kappa symposium on educational research. The beginning researcher is unlikely to be invited to be present and preliminary announcements and programmes are not usually published. The published proceedings can be relied upon to present an up to date review of specialised areas, as well as to indicate likely future growth points. The lists of participants will also be of documentary importance as they include the most advanced researchers in the area, and make a valuable addition to subject headings for searching purposes (*see* chapter 5).

SELECTIVE DISSEMINATION OF INFORMATION (SDI)

Many of the documentary aids mentioned in this chapter use computers to store, sort and print the information. With these systems the output is fixed however, and does not vary from one user to another. The next step in the evolution of computer based systems has been the development of selective dissemination systems where output is individually matched to the interests of each recipient. Many different systems are in operation and the basic principles are discussed in Vickery, B C *Techniques of information retrieval,* Butterworth and Archon Books, 1970, 262 pages.

An example of an SDI system likely to be of use to psychologists is provided by UK MEDLARS (Medical Literative Analysis and Retrieval System). The original system was developed by the US National Library of Medicine to facilitate the more efficient utilisation of the world medical literature, which includes over 2,000 journals as well as many reports, monographs and other publications. All the information in these is scanned by indexers who assign indexing terms from a thesaurus of some 9,000 terms, (*MeSH—medical subject headings*) which is published annually. The bibliographic details of the journal papers, plus the indexing terms are then sorted by computer and produced as the *Index medicus* (a traditional index). The computer also retains this information for subsequent searching and selective dissemination. Whereas a manual search in *Index medicus* has to proceed using only one indexing term at a time, in a computer search by MEDLARS the searcher can specify combinations of terms, and thus receive a unique bibliography which contains only relevant material. For example, to retrieve material on the relationships amongst birth order, laterality, intelligence and behaviour disorders would involve a search under each of these headings separately in each monthly issue of *Index medicus*. While a considerable amount of the information on each single topic may be obtained, the searcher would need to collate all this information to find any relationships. Alternatively, these headings could be specified in a MEDLARS search, together with other headings to limit further the amount of irrelevant material presented (*eg* characteristics found only in preschool children, but not in institutionalised children). The computer print would contain only references where all these terms were found together. After a successful search is completed it can be updated by requesting the computer to supply new information using the same headings. Details of the procedures used are given in Harley, A J *UK medlars: a handbook for users* (second edition), National Lending Library, 1968.

(AMERICAN) NATIONAL INFORMATION SYSTEM FOR PSYCHOLOGY—NISP
The American Psychological Association is developing a comprehensive information system based on the findings of its project on scientific information exchange in psychology (*see* Van Cott, H P 'National Information System for Psychology' *American psychologist*, 1970 25 (5) i-xx). The plans cover three aspects of information flow: primary publication, secondary bibliographic material, and informal information channels.

Four parts of the primary channel are proposed. In highly active research areas information exchange groups will be formed to exchange scientific memoranda. Selective dissemination of information about completed reports will operate through a *Catalog of abstracts*. Any reader will be able to select those reports required from this catalogue, or opt to receive all reports included in one of the selective dissemination channels. This proposal is similar to the existing Experimental

Publication System at present covering organisational behaviour, industrial psychological measurement, special education, educational techniques, family counselling, and vocational and educational guidance. Subdivision of existing journals and the development of new journals will improve the coverage of these publications by matching them more closely to the interests of readers. All manuscripts will be submitted to one central agency, then classified as to the appropriate journal, and followed by editorial review. *Archives of psychology* will publish outstanding work in specific areas, at a frequency determined by the amount of material produced.

At the secondary level, systems for current awareness and browsing will be developed. *Psychological abstracts* will be classified by subject in more depth, with a thesaurus of some 3,000 terms. More information on members' interests will be obtained as part of the *Directory of members,* for use in SDI activities. New informal information channels will be established, and existing channels strengthened. Proposals include audio tape cassettes of lectures by experts, films on therapeutic techniques, and workshops.

The APA do not expect to establish these suggestions overnight, but they will proceed through initial trial period, evaluation and feedback, and subsequent development. Although it is planned to be a national system, one hopes that the benefits may spread to other countries, as did MEDLARS.

DATA BANKS
The ingenious social science researcher can utilise many different kinds of data, ranging from material which has been specially collected via the usual techniques of experiment, observation, questionnaire and interview, to that which is a by-product of societies' everyday functioning, such as records, newspaper reports and personal documents.

The possibility of secondary analysis of such existing data is facilitated by its storage in data banks. Details of many of these, together with literature references, are given in Brittain, J M *Information and its users,* Bath University Press 1970, 208 pages.

FILMS AND OTHER AUDIO-VISUAL MEDIA
Visual media suitable for all ages are covered by the monthly *Visual education.* The British Universities Film Council exists to co-ordinate

the development of film for research and teaching in universities. The *British national film catalogue* is classified so that suitable films may be easily located. Specifically psychological film material is not very extensive. Some useful sources are the British Industrial and Scientific Film Association *Guide to films on psychology and psychiatry* (third edition) 1968, the *Psychological cinema register*, Audio-Visual Services, 6 Willard Building, University Park, Pennsylvania 16802, and Schneider, J M and Kemp, D E *An annotated catalog of films in the behavioral sciences*, Behavioral Science Audio-Visual Laboratory, University of Oklahoma Medical Center. An older guide is Michaelis, A R *Research films in biology, anthropology, psychology and medicine*, Academic Press 1955.

STANDARDS

British Standards (BS) as well as International (ISO) and foreign standards are necessary in engineering and the physical technologies, and relevant ones are of value to the ergonomist and ' hardware ' psychologist, for example, *BS 1404: screen luminance for the projection of 35 mm film on matt and directional screens*. British Standards relevant to documentary work are mentioned in their appropriate contexts throughout this book. Annotated details of British Standards together with a comprehensive subject index are given in the *British Standard yearbook*. The American Psychological Association was a joint sponsor of *Standards for educational and psychological tests and manuals*, 1966, 40 pages.

CHAPTER 5

COMPREHENSIVE SEARCHING SEQUENCES

All stages of empirical research, from the vague initial awareness of the existence of a problem to the testing of specific hypotheses, have their parallel in the comprehensive literature search. It is not possible to divorce the practical problems of a literature search from the theoretical aspects of research, notably the logical requirements for testable hypotheses. The fact that in this chapter the latter are only given passing mention does not indicate that they are not important, but that this chapter is primarily concerned with the practical problems. It is likely that any particular project will only require part of the whole searching sequence. The researcher should select those parts of the sequence which are relevant, using the flow diagram checklist (figure 9).

Many scientific researchers act in a most unscientific way when faced with the problems of conducting a literature search. Many do not search at all, only to find important information at a later stage which, if known in advance, may have altered the whole course of the project. Literature searching and empirical research have much in common, and a problem which has been broken down into its constituent parts for the literature search is likely to be easier to solve by empirical research, which generally requires a similar analysis. Few scientists would consider starting a series of experiments without detailed planning, but they are willing to browse unsystematically in a library when they could benefit by following a planned searching sequence. Similarly, few scientists would publish results without being certain of their accuracy, but literature review and bibliography are not given the same attention. These are just as important as empirical results in the development of science. The researcher who has been fortunate enough to find a good literature review will testify to its value in saving time and effort.

The staff of libraries available to the searcher are likely to be the most important single factor contributing to the success of a search, as they are professionally committed to the maximal efficiency in the utilisation of the library resources. The contribution of their specialised bibliographic knowledge and the searcher's specialised subject knowledge is a potent force to achieve results. It will frequently be necessary to seek their aid and it helps them to assess requirements if they are told why a particular piece of information is needed, as well as what is wanted and how much searching has already been done. As in any type of enquiry asking the right question is the only way to achieve a satisfactory answer.

Five major stages within the comprehensive search may be distinguished: the preliminary groundwork, clarifying the area of enquiry, preparing a bibliography, obtaining and evaluating items, and reporting.

PRELIMINARIES

Methods of searching and the clerical procedures to use in recording the results should be considered before starting the search. Documentary information is frequently recorded in a notebook or on odd scraps of paper, but index cards are recommended, as records need to be handled frequently when inserting new items and adding abstracts and other notes to existing entries. The final layout of the bibliography is rarely clear at the outset and cards can easily be rearranged until an appropriate format is found.

All the bibliographic details of a document should be noted when a reference is first seen, nothing being left to memory. It is important to adopt a consistent order for elements in citations, to save unnecessary transcribing later when the bibliography is being assembled, and to avoid confusion between the various figures which appear in the citation. Unfortunately there is no uniformity within Britain amongst the various primary and secondary sources in their citation practices, in spite of the existence of a *British Standard for bibliographical references* (*BS 1629*). The recommendations of the International Standards Organization (*ISO/R 77*) have not yet been widely accepted internationally, but fortunately many psychological journals use the American Psychological Association system (*see* the *Publication manual* of APA for details). Figure 10 shows the front of a typical reference card. Experience will show that each item of information is of value, particularly to trace a document if a mistake has been made in copying the reference.

Particular care should be taken in transcribing authors' names, as these are frequently used for filing documents and mistakes here

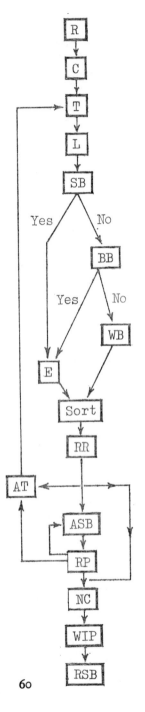

R: Decide how to record information

C: Clarify subject of search

T: Specify retrieval terms

L: Set limits to search

SB: Do you know of a relevant subject bibliography?

BB: Is there anything relevant in bibliographies of bibliography?

WB: Compile a working bibliography

E: Check, extend and/or update subject bibliography

SORT: Sort items into primary and secondary (*ie* review) sources

RR: Retrieve reviews and evaluate

AT: Specify additional retrieval terms

ASB: Add new items to subject bibliography

RP: Retrieve primary sources and evaluate

NC: Make notes and catchword cards

WIP: Check for work in progress

RSB: Write report with relevant subject bibliography

lead to difficulties in location. The order of surname and forenames should be consistent to avoid difficulties such as whether Griffiths W Garvey, is really Griffiths, W Garvey, or Garvey, W Griffiths, or even Garvey-Griffiths, W. Sources will be found to differ in their practices, and a common practice is to put the surname first for the senior author, but forename first for the junior authors. This can lead to difficulties, unless the searcher is aware of this practice, for example BROWN WILLIAM and THOMAS NORMAN, may be BROWN, William and THOMAS, Norman, or BROWN, William and NORMAN, Thomas. Forenames should be transcribed in full, as they are useful in distinguishing between authors in an extensive author index, and also to avoid the later difficulty of confusing the sex of an author, and consequently referring incorrectly to 'his' work. The title of the work should be given in full, and if only a shortened reference is given it is a good idea to write this in pencil until the full title is found.

A standard form for the abbreviation of names of periodicals is given in the *World list of scientific periodicals*. For journal references the full details of date, volume, part, and pages should be given. There might appear to be some redundant information here, but this is a useful safeguard in view of the varying practices of different periodical publishers, and if transcription errors are made the appropriate issue both by date and volume number can be checked. Volume part numbers are useful to libraries that do not bind the whole volume and so are able to lend separate parts. For books the publisher, date, edition (if other than the first), and number of pages should be recorded. The edition is particularly necessary when page references are to be given as these are likely to differ from one edition to the next. The number of pages is useful, as it gives some indication of the size of the work, which may affect the decision whether it is worth examining.

Details of the source of the reference are useful when it is necessary to recheck if it appears to be incorrect—for example the item must have been published before the source of its reference—this information may also be needed by a library when using interlibrary loan facilities. A record of the location and classification details of references available in libraries used by the searcher will save time in rechecking catalogues. An abstract of the document should be written on the reverse of the card, and keywords in title and abstract underlined to facilitate filing by a co-ordinate index system (*see* page 89). In an

FIGURE 10 : Typical reference card

AUTHORS (with first names)	BAYNE Helen	BRY Ilse	127 √	ACTION TAKEN — Accession number of references (for co-ordinate index)
TITLE with keywords underlined for co-ordinate indexing	Problems and projects in the Bibliography of Psychiatry and Psychology			√ = original seen / = references in original noted
JOURNAL	*Libri* 1954 3 ( ) 363-387			
Year				ADDITIONAL INFORMATION
Volume				O = Offprint held
Part				N = Notes held
Pages			N	S = Slide held
SOURCE OF REFERENCE	Walford 2 2nd ed. 13		A02.SSL	+ Location and classification in available libraries.

extensive search, time can be saved by consistently using a code to indicate recurrent themes in an abstract. For example, in a search for material on leadership the various uses of the term ' leader ' may be coded:

L1 = appointed holder of office
L2 = sociometric choice
L3 = group representative
L4 = group co-ordinator.

A research archive should be established to contain notes of every decision taken during the conduct of both empirical and literature research, together with correspondence, press clippings, minutes of meetings, notes of visits, and any other matter which will illuminate the progress of the project. Details such as the scope of the search, bibliographic arrangement, abbreviations, explanations, definitions, which seem obvious at the time may become incomprehensible later when a full account has to be written if no record was kept. Even if not initially required, progress reports will prove a useful discipline to clarify thoughts, and will be invaluable later in showing the directions taken by the project, and the reasons for any changes from the original plan. Ideas peripheral to the main theme come in abundance when one is reading extensively, only to disappear later when further research is being planned. A record of these ideas should be kept, together with a note of the document which stimulated them, so that they can be developed later.

Valuable time can be saved later at the retrieval stages if the idio-syncrasies of the libraries to be used are learned at the outset. For example, what kind of catalogue is available, how are books on order recorded, are there any special or reserve collections of books, what about oversize books, back files of periodicals, is there a vertical file for pamphlets and press clippings? Rapid reading and the ability to skim the essentials from a document are useful skills to develop in view of the mass of material to be evaluated.

CLARIFYING THE AREA OF ENQUIRY

All research starts with the awareness of a problem. This may just be a vague idea that research upon a certain topic is necessary, or may be the knowledge of a specific hypothesis, or at any point between these extremes. In all cases it is necessary at the outset to read widely around the problem to illuminate all facets of it. The specificity with which the problem can be stated at this stage will influence the depth and amount of preliminary background reading which is necessary. Exploratory research intended to clarify variables and develop hypotheses will start with the searcher having little knowledge, and consequently the preliminary reading must range widely so as not to miss any fruitful insights. With research to test a well developed hypothesis there is a temptation to assume that background reading is unnecessary. This is a dangerous assumption, as it is easy to become too narrowly circumscribed and miss new ideas from related areas. Any problem is likely to have several facets, *eg labour turnover* related to *family structure* and *age* of worker; each facet is a subdivision of a larger class, such as *mobility, kinship, gerontology,* and each facet may appear independently in other contexts, *eg labour turnover* and size of firm, *family structure* and social class, *age* and memory. Insight into the problem can be gained both from the larger classes and other contexts.

Preliminary reading should be conducted with a broad approach, with textbooks, handbooks, encyclopedias and the like being used to give a balanced viewpoint. Details of such books can be obtained from bibliographies and book reviews (*see* chapter 4 for details). If the searcher finds that these sources do not add significantly to his existing knowledge of the area, then review articles at the next level of sophistication should be sought. Any relevant specific references should of course be noted, but the object at this stage is not to discover these, but to set the general background to the search. At the end of this period of general introduction, it should be possible to state clearly the relevant variables or topics which will provide the framework for comprehensive search.

A hierarchy of searching terms should be developed from the topics and variables generated by the general introductory reading. Use of a dictionary of psychology and a thesaurus will indicate terms and synonyms and various meanings of these searching terms. The hierarchy developed should range from the most general to the highly specific terms, and include as many synonyms as can be generated at each level. The more extensive this list can be made at the outset, the less the likelihood of the searcher having to retrace his steps through secondary sources already covered, when new terms are later found. Searching terms and synonyms will be clarified by reference to the classification system used in the library, which may indicate that aspects of the topic may be found under other subject headings. Terms will also be revealed by checking the indexes to the major abstracting systems to be used.

Names of prominent specialists in the area of enquiry should also be noted, and these may be used for searching. Extreme care is essential when using names of people and things for searching, however, as variations and changes in the names may occur from place to place and from time to time. These may particularly result from differences in transliteration of Russian and other non-European alphabets (*see* chapter 8), transcription errors, marriage, migration to a different country and similar circumstances. Different alphabetical orders may also be found, for example most searchers could be ready to look under different locations for ' Mc ' and ' Mac ' but might find difficulty with ä—often filed under ae, or Å—as A in English sources, but after z in Norwegian and before A in Danish. A useful guide to foreign alphabets is given in ' Foreign alphabetization practices ' by Ernst Van Hagen (pages 505-509, in Industrial and Engineering Chemistry *Literature resources for chemical process industries; Advances in chemistry,* number 10 (1954), American Chemical Society, Washington).

In addition to the list of search terms, a list of documentary aids to be used in the search should be compiled. This list also should range from the most general, *ie* tertiary sources to the highly specific, *ie* primary sources—see figure 4. Sufficient space should be left next to each item to accommodate notes of the volume numbers checked and the search terms used. Library holdings lists of periodicals are useful for finding details of relevant sources, but may lead to some confusion by their layout. Journals may be listed under the name of a society, such as *British Psychological Society—bulletin,* or *American Statistical Association—journal,* whereas other periodicals are listed in the straightforward manner (*Journal of personality*).

A note of the hypotheses, variables, and the scope of the project should be kept with these lists, and consulted frequently to avoid running off into interesting but irrelevant sidetracks. The lone researcher will be acting both as initiator of the enquiry and searcher, and as these roles are frequently separate in library searching, the researcher should ensure that the objectives of the search are clear.

65

3

Discussing these objectives with somebody who does not have specialised knowledge of the topic may help to clarify them, because answering ' naive ' questions helps to show gaps and unstated assumptions. Are these objectives to find as much as one can that has been written about a topic, or will a selection of relevant articles be sufficient? In what ways are the scope of the search to be limited; is conceptual, procedural, or empirical information sought; are there any language or national limits; what historical limits, and in particular is there a base date beyond which it is unnecessary to search?

Before starting the detailed search it is useful to check how long it will take to compile the bibliography, to locate and evaluate the documents and to write the report. Some idea of the amount of material and its scatter through the various sources can be obtained by conducting a pilot check in relevant secondary sources. If this indicates a large mass of material, then it may be necessary to limit the scope of the search, particularly if there is only limited time available for its completion. It is easy to underestimate the time required for a truly comprehensive search. It would not be over emphasising the importance of searching to suggest that of the total time budget for a research project up to one third should be spent in documentary work, which will include the literature report.

PREPARING THE BIBLIOGRAPHY

There are alternative routes to the goal of a subject bibliography but a useful general rule is to start by searching with the most specific search terms in the most general source. A bibliography of bibliographies will reveal any relevant subject bibliography. Any subject bibliography found should indicate the criteria used for inclusion of material, both by time and subject matter, and it will need to be checked for adequacy and brought up to date. The adequacy can be checked by sampling indexes and abstracts for the period covered by the bibliography and noting whether all the relevant items in these are listed in it. If serious gaps are found then a full comprehensive search as shown below will be necessary. The searcher will rarely find a completely up to date subject bibliography and so it will be necessary to add more recent material by using relevant secondary sources such as abstracts and indexes, or by scanning primary material such as journals not covered by secondary sources. When the research topic is within the coverage of MEDLARS or the *Science citation index*, these will form powerful tools in preparing or updating a bibliography (*see* chapter 4).

In the absence of an existing subject bibliography, the searcher has to compile his own by using the appropriate secondary sources which will generally be abstracts and/or indexes. A complete bibliography can rarely be compiled from abstracts alone, however, because of gaps in the coverage of even the best of these, and so any relevant primary sources in the list of documents previously compiled which are not covered in this way will have to be checked individually. The search process thus involves moving down the hierarchy of sources towards the primary material, but it should be rarely necessary to operate solely at this level.

It is sometimes possible to establish a base date, with documents published before this time being of little value. This base might be the introduction of a concept, or the date of comprehensive review of the area. When such a base can be established, it is advisable to work backwards in time towards it from current material. In this way the relevance of older material is continually checked against the more recent, and the search concluded when the yield becomes sparse either in quantity or in quality. Another signal to conclude the search comes when a large proportion of the references being found have already been noted. A good bibliography does not necessarily include everything written about the topic, but that which the compiler considers to be relevant to his stated criteria. It is impossible to find everything which might be relevant, and the costs of extra effort at this point will generally outweigh the benefits.

Two general methods of searching may be distinguished: by using documentary aids as outlined above, and by 'snowballing' (using references in a current paper to generate further references, and checking these to yield yet further references, and so on). Snowballing is frequently used, but it has severe weaknesses in that it depends upon the extent of knowledge and the citation practices of authors. It is known that they often tend to be parochial, ignoring work in a foreign language, or even research conducted outside their own laboratory. If used, the snowballing method should be supplemented by documentary aids. A variant of the snowballing method is the use of the 'old boy network'. Details of work in progress and papers awaiting publication in the journal pipelines are likely to be known to experts in each specific area as a consequence of their personal contacts. They are usually willing to help the beginning researcher who indicates the extent of his present knowledge and who specifies exactly what kind of information is wanted.

The end product of this stage of preparing a bibliography will be a large number of reference cards, including many which will be found to be irrelevant. It may be possible to weed out any duplicates. Unfortunately, the same material is likely to be published in more than one form, thus increasing the problems of the searcher. One frequently finds, for example, that preliminary findings were presented at a conference, then a journal paper published, and a report published by a sponsoring agency. Different emphasis may be placed upon the work in these publications depending upon the interests of the different target audiences. The latest or most extensive publication may be used alone unless there is reason to suppose that earlier ones contain material not duplicated later. This is often the case with higher degree theses, with the thesis being valuable for its literature review, whereas papers produced from it tend to concentrate upon empirical findings.

RETRIEVAL AND EVALUATION

Items in the bibliography may be divided at this stage into reviews and original findings. One should attempt to retrieve reviews first, as they give a good overall view of the topic, and then original findings should fit into the pattern. A bibliography listed on cards can be rearranged to bring together all references to a particular source or in a given location, thus saving time when retrieving documents. Most libraries will not contain all the documents needed, and the searcher will need to consult his librarian about interlibrary lending facilities. Occasionally it will not be possible for a library to obtain a document, and then the searcher will have to consider travelling to a library where it is available.

As the documents are retrieved they should be skimmed to check that they are within the scope of the project, and if so then evaluated upon two criteria; the contents—does it contain useful ideas, methods or data?; and the references—is there anything relevant which has not already been found during the preparation of the bibliography? The reference card should be marked when the contents have been evaluated, and further marked when all references have been checked. It is essential to try and obtain every document which appears to be relevant, and not to rely upon information given in abstracts or reviews. The original will frequently be found to have a different slant from that which might have been inferred from a summary, and misconceptions are easily communicated by scientists reporting without seeing the originals. If the original cannot be obtained, and it appears to deal with an important point, then details may be included in the report, but a note should be also included that the original was not seen.

Sufficiently detailed notes of the contents of each document should be made to enable a report to be written without further reference to the original. The discipline involved in writing an abstract is a useful check that one fully understands the documents. Where an item is of central importance, a copy may be retained, but one should beware of establishing too large a file of offprints. It does not help to duplicate the library in one's own records! The co-ordinate index system (*see* chapter 8) is recommended to enable quick retrieval of notes and offprints when needed for reporting.

A set of small cards may be found useful to note ideas as they develop during evaluation. Details should be kept as brief as possible, merely including the key words of an idea and a reference to the relevant document. It is essential to differentiate between quotations from a document and one's own ideas which come as the result of reading the document, since it may not be clear at a later date which is which, with the consequent danger of plagiarisation. This danger can be avoided by consistently using quotation marks and indicating omissions (. . .) and putting paraphrased ideas within square brackets [ ].

When documents are found which appeared to be relevant from their title, but which in fact are of no interest, this point together with reasons should be noted and the reference card retained. It is important not to destroy these ' useless ' records, because in an extensive search the reference may later be found again and time wasted on re-retrieval and evaluation if the original record was destroyed and forgotten. It should not be necessary to remind psychologists that memory is fallible.

At the end of the evaluation stage the searcher will have two sets of cards: reference cards with full details and abstracts; and ideas cards showing key ideas around which the literature report may be constructed. Retrieval and evaluation will need to continue during report writing and empirical work, as new material will be continually emerging.

After evaluating the literature, there is a natural temptation to get on with empirical research based upon it, without making any report of the literature. This temptation should be resisted because it is far easier to draft a report on documents recently evaluated than to recall details after an intervening time spent on empirical research. The type of report of the search will depend upon the purpose of the project, *eg* for higher degree thesis, or journal paper, or practical problem posed by an organisation, and upon the extent and originality of the area of search. The searcher should always consider publishing the literature review and bibliography so as to save the duplication of effort involved by other researchers who may wish to follow him. The findings of a literature search may be the most valuable product of a research project, and should be considered independently of the empirical findings, particularly as these two products are likely to be used by different people and for different purposes. Reputations have been built on good literature surveys, particularly those of the level of *Psychological bulletin* and *Annual review of psychology*.

The report writer should always consider the needs of his readers, and construct the report accordingly. A chronological development of the topic is easiest to write, but is not the best from the point of view of a user who may only be interested in one aspect of the topic. A more generally useful structure collects together information from many diverse sources, and discusses it facet by facet. Whatever structure of report is to be used, the writer first needs to construct an outline plan. This can be developed by sorting the 'idea' cards into various sets until an appropriate structure emerges. The reference cards relating to each aspect can then be collected together and a section drafted from the abstracts on them. Only relevant material should be included. A show of knowledge for its own sake or as a demonstration that an extensive search was conducted merely serves to irritate the reader seeking the salient points. The searcher who has been frustrated by having to deal with material where the title did not adequately reflect the contents will not need reminding about the importance of a suitable fully descriptive title. The scope, limits and objectives of the search should be clearly indicated, so that the reader will know exactly where expansion may be necessary. Attention should also be given to the format of the bibliography. Items should be numbered for ease of reference, and a list of contents or index may be necessary for all but the most short simple bibliography.

CHAPTER 6

CURRENT AWARENESS

All the effort expended on the comprehensive search can be wasted if the searcher does not keep his information up to date. An individual's use of current awareness represents his evaluation of the use to him of other people's work. At one extreme are those so supremely confident in the originality of their own work, or so supremely indifferent to the contribution of others, that they find no need to keep up to date with the literature. At the other extreme are those who spend so much time in keeping up with others that insufficient time is left for their own empirical work. The ideal state is somewhere between these two extremes.

Current awareness must be undertaken in a systematic manner. Time should be set aside each week or month to keep up with the literature, otherwise this task is easily forgotten, and an increasing pile of unread material becomes a daunting task. An individual may find that checking the current copy of *Psychological abstracts* gives sufficient information about the literature in his areas of interest, whereas another person may prefer to scan the current copies of periodicals which specialise in his field, much will depend upon his experience of the adequacy of coverage of these methods. *Current contents, in behavioral, social and management sciences* and similar periodicals which reprint the contents pages of current journals are a useful aid, in bringing together a range of information which can be quickly scanned (*see* chapter 4 for details). A librarian who knows the searcher's range of interests can be invaluable by drawing attention to new material which might otherwise be missed.

A group may find the idea of a journal club useful; each person undertakes to scan a number of journals and keep all the others informed of relevant developments. This assumes, of course, that all members are able and willing to specify the range of their interests. Computer based selective dissemination of information (SDI) systems work in a similar manner: the researcher selects a number of keywords which represents his interests from the thesaurus used for content analysis of the incoming information. He is then alerted by the computer whenever a document is classified under the relevant keywords (*see* chapter 4).

In addition to keeping up with the literature, the researcher will want to know what other people are doing in their current research, to ensure that his work does not unintentionally duplicate it. Some researchers are reluctant to reveal work in progress, but information or clues can be gained from a variety of sources, without resorting to industrial espionage! Time spent in report writing together with the publication lag can frequently mean that by the time material is published it no longer represents what an individual is currently doing. Some journals are aware of this problem, and print lists of papers accepted for publication, together with author's address, and thus one can get relevant information in advance of publication. Scientific work increasingly requires funds, and the reports of grant awarding bodies may be useful to give early information about work in progress. The *SSRC newsletter* gives information about grants awarded, not only by SSRC but also by other bodies supporting social research. Other newsletters devoted to specific areas (*see* appendix D for details) and miscellaneous news items in journals which are the official organs of the various psychological societies such as *Bulletin of the British Psychological Society* and the *American psychologist*, may also provide leads.

In addition to the general directories of research in progress, some subject areas appear to be particularly aware of the dangers of unplanned duplication of effort, and attempt to register work in progress. For example, the annual *Training research register* (HMSO) gives details of current and recently completed research projects closely related to training. Education in the UK has the NFER *Register of current researches in education*, and in the US *Phi delta kappan* includes regular ' Doctors Theses under way in Education ', and the Educational Research Information Center (ERIC) holds reports of projects in progress.

Conference material can also be a fertile source of clues, and the informal gossip during conferences will often indicate work being planned, grants applied for, and similar early information. Advertisements of staff vacancies and announcements of appointments may provide clues of the development of research, and relevant specialists. Many departments of psychology now indicate the research interests of individual staff members when advertising vacancies for graduate research students (*see* for example, the British Psychological Society

73

Appointments memorandum). Everyday sources of news, such as newspapers, radio and TV should not be ignored. These may reveal details of work in progress which has not yet reached a sufficiently advanced level for dissemination to the scientific community.

CHAPTER 7

EVERYDAY REFERENCE ENQUIRIES

Whereas in comprehensive search and current awareness one attempts to be exhaustive in covering a topic, everyday references enquiries have the limited objective of finding answers to specific questions. Questions differ in their specificity, but this cannot always be discerned at the outset. Some questions have only one correct answer. For example, the address of the secretary of an organisation, or the formula for a statistical calculation, can quickly be obtained from a directory or handbook. Other questions can have several answers, but one may be better than others: for example, data on the incidence of mental illness or a statement of Freud's view on thanatos. Questions of this type will require some preliminary searching to reveal the most reliable or up to date source: how are data on mental illness compiled and where are they published; is there a standard commentary on Freud which will obviate the need to browse through the collected works? A third type of question can be answered from several acceptable points of view: for example, what are the determinants of the shape of a learning curve; or the facets of leadership behaviour? This type of question could lead to very extensive searches, and so will need to be clarified and reduced in scope.

With all types of questions, however, time taken to analyse the problem will save time otherwise spent in fruitless searching. Is the question as specific as possible? Are all the terms completely unambiguous, can the question be further simplified by employing Kipling's ' six good serving men '; what, who, when, where, how, why? Do associated facts need to be found to set the information in context?

As in the comprehensive searching procedure, it is best to start searching in tertiary and secondary sources, such as guides, directories, handbooks, encyclopedias, and reviews. Empirical and procedural information will generally be located in this way, but conceptual information is often more difficult to pin down. Even the question may be more difficult to state, but browsing through the subject index of relevant books may provide leads.

If the literature available locally does not provide the answer, then it will be necessary to range more widely. One may be reasonably confident that a particular reference book will give the information, but libraries are reluctant to lend such material. Would a telephone or telex enquiry settle the problem? Specialist libraries, clearing houses, information exchanges, and many research organisations which may be located through directories are willing to answer specific questions.

Some reference questions have much in common with detective work. Finding an address is generally simple, but there can be problems particularly with mobile academics. A person may not be a member of the appropriate professional organisation, or the obvious directory may be out of date. An organisational affiliation given in a recent scientific paper can be useful in these cases. This approach located a psychologist whose name did not appear in the *APA directory*, although he was known to have worked in an American university. His latest publication, abstracted in *Psychological abstracts*, indicated a Czech address which proved to be correct.

One may remember reading a report, but fail to find details in one's reference system. Who re-analysed the data on children's morality from *Studies in the nature of character* by Hartshorn and May, and came to a different conclusion from the original one? A re-analysis which reversed the conclusions of a classic study should certainly have been mentioned in a review, and the reviewer would very probably cite the original reference. The author index to each issue of *Annual review of psychology* was checked, and this gave a few citations of Hartshorn. Details of the wanted reference (Burton R V 'Generality of honesty reconsidered' *Psychological review*, 1963 70, pages 481-499) were found within Holtzman's review of personality structure in volume 16 of the *Annual review of psychology*.

When the search appears to be yielding neither answers nor clues, one should stop to consider why. Rarely will a subject be so obscure as not to have had some research attention. Could the topic have been covered under a different name, *eg* PGR or GSR? Is checking by author likely to be worthwhile if a subject approach has failed? This depends upon the adequacy of one's existing information and the availability of indexes in available sources. When the author's name is known, but searching under this is fruitless, it may be worthwhile checking whether the work was conducted in or for an organisation, and using this as 'author' entry. Is it the kind of problem that nobody has thought sufficiently important to record, but which the expert practitioner would have at his fingertips (such as how to operate a specific piece of equipment)? What gave rise to the problem? Could it be tackled in a different way? Is the problem sufficiently important to merit a comprehensive search, or must the answer be found immediately to be of any use?

Even when an apparent answer is found, it is essential to check and double check it. Information is not necessarily correct merely because it is printed. For example published data may be copied at several removes from the original publication, with consequent likelihood of transcription errors, rounding off of data, selection of partial information and loss of notes on method of compilation. On the other hand figures are sometimes revised when better data are subsequently obtained, and so later official sources may give better data than the information published close to an event. Once a reference problem has occurred, there is a strong likelihood of the same question recurring, and so information of the answer found and sources used should be kept in the personal reference file.

CHAPTER 8

MISCELLANEOUS INFORMATION PROBLEMS

BOOK SELECTION AND EVALUATION
The selection and evaluation of books is frequently a collaborative task for the librarian and the subject specialist, and each can bring their individual skills to bear on the problem. The librarian will have specialised sources for learning about forthcoming books, such as the national and trade bibliographies, but the output of books in all areas is so great that some may be missed and most librarians appreciate help. The specialist can particularly help by notifying the librarian of books published by sources other than the usual commercial publishers, pamphlets and other ephemeral material. Book reviews are the major sources of evaluative information but as these take time to be prepared and published, they may be late in appearing relative to the publication of the book. In addition to this there appears to be a considerable time lag between the announcement of publication of books in the US and their appearance in UK. *Contemporary psychology* is the major source of book reviews in psychology, but other journals carry reviews of works in their specialised areas (for book review sources *see* appendix E).

In evaluating a book, one has to consider first the purpose that one intends it to serve: a textbook will need to satisfy different criteria from those required by a reference work. Is the textbook intended as the main source for a course, or as supplementary material; for what level of student; what are the objectives of the course; what experience of the subject will students have had before using the book; how well motivated are they; etc.

Is the reference book the only one to serve the topic, or to supplement others; what kind of reference questions are likely to be asked, *eg* different in an undergraduate teaching department when compared with a research institute. One should try not to be biased by one's own specialist view of the subject unless the book was specifically intended for a person with this specialist knowledge.

An overall evaluation is based upon a synthesis of impressions about a book, to which the following areas are likely to contribute. The title should accurately reflect the contents of the whole work, and distinguish it from any similar books. A book by a single author should reveal a more consistent style though it may contain varying levels of competence in the different aspects of the topic. Multiple authors, on the other hand, should have been selected for their individual competence, although it is sometimes doubtful whether this is the case, it being more likely that they are merely known to each other. What proportion of the total was contributed by each author, and has a ' big name ' simply been used as a sales device? How far has an editor or compiler tried to impose his own style and viewpoint upon the contributors, with the positive virtue of a consistent work, but the associated danger of unsuitable standardisation? Is the author well known in the specialised field? This has the advantage that one could expect a particular viewpoint or leaning—for example one would not expect a sympathetic treatment of psychoanalysis from a behaviourist. On the other hand, the unknown person is likely to have devoted more attention to the work in order to be accepted by the publisher, whereas the 'big name' author may be living off his past success. What is the author's background of training and experience, both research and practical, and how does this particularly fit or hinder him in the treatment of the material?

Is the publisher known to specialise in the relevant area, with the advantage of experienced staff to assist in the production of the work? What level are other books produced by this publisher? Again there is the possibility that established publishers are unwilling to take the risks necessarily attendant upon doing something new, and so an unknown publisher is not necessarily a bad thing. In this specialised business there are many different approaches, from the quick profit by vast sales of popular works to the prestige imprints: the American textbook market is so vast that these can be produced in great variety, but one should be wary of pseudo-reference works whose only virtue is an income for author and publisher.

The date of writing is necessarily some time before the date of publication, because of production time, and so the recency of the material cannot be determined fully by publication date, nor by any date given in the author's introduction, which is usually the last to be written. A check should be made of the material in the list of references or bibliography; what is the latest date of material there? Is there any more recent material which could have been expected to appear? Some directories merely compile material existing in other directories, thus compounding errors and out of date information. Accuracy may be evaluated by checking a reasonable sample of material of which the reviewer has specialised knowledge (for example details of my own university given in *Minerva: jahrbuch der gelehrten Welt* were found to be at least two years out of date on publication, thus casting doubt on the accuracy of the rest of the material). The balance of treatment of aspects of the topic should be considered both in terms of the amount of space devoted to them and the accuracy and recency of the material. Controversial material should be indicated as such in a text-book, and both sides of the controversy presented.

The preface or introduction should at least indicate the intended readership, the purpose of the book, the reason why the author considered such a book necessary and details of any special features. Has a textbook been tried out on the type of student for which it is intended? Does it contain questions which have also been tested, and does it provide answers? Is the author correct that such a book is needed; when compared with others on the same subject does it add anything in material or presentation, or merely 'rehash' existing works? If a textbook promises a range of supplementary material such as instructor's guide and test material, are those available now, or at some hopeful time in the future?

Some publishers attempt to suggest the success of a book by stressing that it has had a second (or further) reprint. This should be viewed with caution as it may indicate a deliberate policy of small print orders, although this is more frequent in works of fiction than in reference material. A second or later edition indicates that the first edition was sufficiently well received to justify it, but the two editions should be compared. Is 'second edition' merely a sales device, or are there substantial changes—the latter should be pointed out in the author's introduction. Has the format of the book changed as necessitated by the development of the subject *eg* many textbooks still assume a three-fold split of the subject matter of psychology.

The crucial check of any book is its ease of usage. The index can be evaluated by asking questions and checking the ease with which they may be answered: is the index sufficiently detailed or too detailed with respect to the length and subject matter of the work? Do cross references help, or merely send the reader into an infinite loop? Are there appropriate examples in the text to clarify and illuminate abstract concepts or is there unnecessary repetition and padding? How long does it take to read and understand a sample section, and how does it compare with time taken for comparable material? (The computation of a readability index, such as the Fleisch index, may help to quantify impressions.) Are diagrams, graphs and other illustrations clearly labelled, and is their meaning clear without reference to the text? Do tables balance? Have percentages been computed in the correct direction. Are sources of material quoted? Are illustrations necessary, do they add anything apart from length to the book? Does the layout of chapters or sections follow a logical sequence and is this explained in the introduction? Does the layout within chapters invite further reading, with sufficient summaries, subheadings, etc? What does the extent of references, both temporal and geographical, tell about the author's view of the subject? The physical condition of the book will rarely be relevant from the viewpoint of user evaluation, but the librarian will want to be sure that it will withstand the use expected of it.

REPORT WRITING

The research report, be it written or spoken, is the most common means of dissemination of ideas, and an assessment of the quality of these ideas is influenced by the quality of their communication.

Communication skills need practice just like any other skill, and they do not come easily to many researchers. Several books about the techniques of writing and speaking are available, and they will repay careful study. The most common difficulty is to aspire to write the finished work at the first attempt, whereas even experienced authors find it necessary to progress through several drafts. Preparation and collection of all the material is essential before starting to write, as the creative flow is easily inhibited by having to stop and check results, references, etc. The purpose of the report and the level of ability, knowledge, and interest of the target audience should be considered at the outset, since these will influence the type of report to be written. The ideas to be communicated should be ordered into a logical sequence and an outline plan drawn up. It often helps if a report of empirical work can be drafted whilst the work is still in progress, as drafting the report may bring to light inconsistencies and side issues which can be examined whilst equipment and subjects are still available.

Once the material has been collected and the plan developed, the first draft should be written as quickly as possible, not stopping to think of the most appropriate word nor worrying about grammar but simply capturing the ideas. The completed first draft should be left aside long enough for it to be seen in a coldly critical light, and then revisions made to the grammar, style and mode of expression. These two aspects of creative construction and critical evaluation should not be attempted at the same time, as they require entirely different states of mind. Clarity and brevity are the twin ideals for any report, and these can only be achieved by practice and the feedback of criticism from colleagues.

Written reports

Submission for publication implies that it is original work, and not under consideration elsewhere, and that if accepted it will not be submitted elsewhere, in any language, without editorial approval. The style of presentation will depend upon the house style of the publisher, and this should be checked at the outset. Many publishers supply style manuals, but if these are not available, then the layout of the target journal should be studied and a general style manual, such as the Royal Society *General notes on the preparation of scientific papers,* or Turabain, K L *A manual for writers* consulted. A typist who knows the layout required can relieve the author of much routine drafting, and so a specimen copy of the relevant journal should be given to her together with the manuscript. Much can be done to make the article appealing to the eye by using subheadings, and breaking the material into sections. A direct writing style using short sentences, and simple expressions helps the reader and will increase the chances of the paper being read.

With the increasing use of computers for indexing it has become even more necessary to ensure that the title adequately indicates the content of the paper. Each word should be examined to ensure that it is a suitable keyword for retrieval purposes and that there are no redundancies. A summary should be able to stand on its own and make sense to a person who had not read the paper, but who possesses some knowledge of the general subject area. The introduction should outline the background of the topic, evaluate previous relevant research, indicate any special treatment of the topic, and clearly delineate the area covered. Any practical problems or symptoms which initiated the research should be analysed into their constituent parts, and hypotheses and assumptions stated with operational definitions of all terms. New terms should only be coined when they are really necessary and not merely to introduce jargon for its own sake. Techniques used, including selection of subjects, should be reported in sufficient detail for the reader to replicate the research and should be appropriate to the original problem with any unusual modifications justified. Units of measurement for all variables must be clearly stated and the data obtained must be sufficient to test the hypothesis.

Results will rarely be given in full, but the reader must have access to the raw data if necessary. The NLL supplementary publications scheme or the SSRC data bank may be used. Most tables of results could be presented in more than one way (*see* Zeisel, H *Say it with figures*) and the various alternatives should be considered bearing in mind the size of the journal page. A small table has a greater probability of being read, and so the author should consider whether everything he intends to put in it is really essential. Tables should be numbered, given an informative heading, and be referred to by number within the text. Zero results should be distinguished from conditions where observations were not made, and the number of significant figures indicate the level of accuracy of the data, *eg* differences between 5, 5·0 and 5·00, in the accuracy implied. Tables and graphs of the same results are rarely accepted, and so the clearest manner of presentation should be sought, bearing in mind that graphs may be reduced to fit the page and so what was clear in the original may become confused in a reproduction. Any breaks in the scales should be clearly indicated, and distinctions made between theoretical and empirical findings. Mathematical symbols cause difficulty for typist and printer alike, and so they must be carefully checked. Conclusions must be shown to be valid on the basis of the evidence presented in the paper, and alternative conclusions similarly rejected. Conclusions must also be related to the problems raised in the introduction, together with limitations and qualifications to their generality. References should be relevant, and not just to indicate the extent of the literature searching.

Printers' proofs are solely to check that the manuscript has been correctly set and so only alterations resulting from printers' errors are legitimate, and authors must generally pay for any other alterations. Only standard proof correction symbols as given in *British standard 1219* should be used.

Conference papers

(*See* Cook, E B ' Oral presentation of a scientific paper ', pages 150-166 in Woodford, F P *Scientific writing for graduate students,* Macmillan 1968, 190 pages.) Papers presented orally serve different objectives to those intended for publication. The conference paper will primarily stake the author's claim and whet the appetite of the audience for more details. In addition to this any members of the audience can contact the speaker after his presentation. Both kinds of paper need to be prepared with the same amount of care and as the conference will provide immediate feedback the author will need to be more sure of his topic than when he is screened from his audience by an editor and cold print. An audience will sympathise with slight nervousness on the part of the speaker, but he should speak slowly and clearly and avoid mannerisms.

In addition to organising the ideas and polishing the draft, it is essential to ensure that the paper can be presented in the time available. This means that it must be read aloud at the speed of presentation to be used, which will be slower than normal speech and considerably slower than silent reading speed. The paper intended for publication is not suitable for oral presentation, as there is a lower limit to the amount of information that the audience can absorb. Simplicity is the keynote to a good oral paper. Only a few new ideas should be presented at a time, with repetition of the important points allowing time for them to be digested. Results should be kept to a minimum, with simple graphs which are easier to understand than tables. The presentation of visual aids will need to be coordinated with the paper, and a copy of the paper should be available incorporating clear cues for a projectionist. The conditions of illumination and magnification for visual aids should be ascertained to ensure that all details will be clear to all the audience. Handouts should have all sections clearly labelled, and be referred to by section number during presentation of the paper.

Preparing an index to a book is a complementary task to that of compiling a bibliography. The latter task involves synthesising diverse elements to form an integrated whole, whereas the former involves an objective analysis of the text to reveal all its facets. *British Standard 3700* makes recommendations for the content, construction, arrangement and preparation of indexes, and outlines basic indexing principles and practice. A useful basic text is Collison, R L *Indexing books,* Benn, 1962. Although many authorities recommend that indexing is best done by a specialist indexer with the help of the author to determine appropriate subject headings, most authors undertake this task on their own. Psychologists familiar with content analysis will find much in common between the two operations.

All the text, including footnotes and appendices, should be meticulously analysed to determine the words to be used as entries in the index, with thought being given to the manner in which the reader is likely to approach the subject matter. For example, is the reader likely to use terms from everyday speech (' nervous breakdown ') or technical terms (' neurosis '). This will depend upon the readership to which the book is aimed and, if a heterogeneous readership is likely, then it will be necessary to provide cross references from everyday to technical language. Each entry, together with its page reference(s), should be written on a small card or slip of paper. Page references should be given in full. For example, if a reference covers more than one page, then the first and last pages are given. After all the text has been analysed the entries will need to be arranged into a suitable order. The questions of arrangement—either letter-by-letter or word-by-word (*see* chapter 2)—and whether to form separate subject and name indexes or a combined index, have to be settled at the outset.

Entries should be classified into superordinate and subordinate categories to yield an index with main headings and subheadings as well as possible sub-subheadings. A heading will need to be subdivided when it contains references to material at several different places in the book. Most authorities recommend that no entry should have more than four page references. Under each main heading the division into subheadings must be mutually exclusive. For example, given:

Learning
    Theory
    Programmed

the reader would not know where to find theoretical work on programmed learning. This can be avoided by using one as a subheading
of the other:

Learning
    Theory
        Programmed

Two kinds of cross reference will be required. ' *See* ' *cross references*
direct the reader from a heading which does not have page references
to an alternative heading where the relevant references are given:

eg Manifest anxiety scale, *see* Tests

.

.

.

.

Tests
    Army general classification test 160-161

.

.

.

.

    Manifest anxiety scale 132, 137, 140-143.

' *See also* ' *cross references* direct the reader from a heading to additional headings where further references are given: *eg* Hypotheses 57,
211, 219, *see also* Statistical tests.

TRANSLATIONS

Evidence of the parochialism of many scientists is given by the low
level of citations of foreign language material, and surveys which show
that they rarely read material in foreign languages. This has dangers
of unplanned duplication of effort and in the absence of a reading
knowledge of foreign languages, the availability of translations is the
next best thing.

Detailed translation of scientific documents is time consuming and
thus costly, and so it is regrettable that the same document may be
translated more than once because the user does not know of the

existence of a translation. Librarians have attempted to reduce this possibility by compiling centralised indexes of existing translations and of work in progress. ASLIB maintains an index to English translations of articles in all languages, and covering many subjects, but with emphasis on science and technology (*Commonwealth index to unpublished translations*). Information is collected from over 300 organisations in the UK and from the principal Commonwealth countries at the rate of some 12,000 each year. Some languages are likely to cause more trouble than others, for example the searcher may remember a smattering of his schoolboy French, and this may be sufficient to convey the gist of an article, but oriental and cyrillic languages are far more difficult. When faced with an article in one of these languages, it is useful to know that the European Translations Centre (Delft-Netherlands) publish a quarterly index of translations from non-western into western languages (*ETC world index*).

When a foreign document is located, one must attempt to find out specifically what aspects of the topic are covered, at what level, and whether it is important enough to merit a full translation. Some idea of these can be found from abstracts, comments or citations by reliable authors, and by a systematic check of the document itself. Formulae, graphs, and diagrams are usually relatively easy to understand in most languages, and a dictionary can be used to translate critical portions such as summaries, details of method, and results. References cited may give an indication of the recency of the material. Transliteration of Russian, Hebrew and other languages will be necessary as an aid to the use of the dictionary, and British and International systems for transliteration are available. (*British Standard 2979* for Cyrillic and Greek; *ISO/R 233* for Arabic; *ISO/R 259* for Hebrew.)

Difficulties are likely to arise when a name had been transliterated twice. For example Hoseh* cites a case where a Czech author *Capek* was transliterated into Russian as Чапек and then into English as *Chapek*. Thus his name may be found in an English source as either *Capek* or *Chapek*. Even more confusing is the situation where a Russian name could be transliterated into various Western European languages

---

* Hoseh, M ' Pitfalls of transliteration in indexing and searching ' pages 541-547, in Industrial and Engineering Chemistry *Literature resources for chemical process industries,* Advances in chemistry, no 10 (1954), American Chemical Society Washington.

and appear quite different because of attempts to reproduce the original sound. Thus *Shadanow, Jdanoff,* and *Zhdanov,* would be the German, French and English transliterations of the same Russian name : Жданов. The original language is usually obvious, or may be guessed from the place of publication, but in doubtful cases, particularly closely related languages, a language identification handbook may be necessary (*see* appendix н).

Some journals are translated in their entirety ('cover to cover' translations). Details of these may be found in *Technical translations* (us Government Printing Office); for example : *Referativynyi zhurnal kibernetika* becomes *Cybernetics abstracts.* Other journals consist of collections of translations from a variety of foreign periodicals (*see* appendix c).

Most psychologists are familiar with communication experiments which show that one way communication is likely to result in error, because the originator may not be able to express his ideas accurately and the receiver may misunderstand fine nuances in these expressed ideas because of the limitations of the language. These errors are likely to be further compounded by the insertion of a translator into the communication channel. The original may be unclear; the translator may mistake the finer shades of meaning particularly if he is not familiar with the subject matter; it may be impossible to express the exact meaning of the original language in English, *eg gestalt;* the translator may express himself badly; and the reader may mistake the meaning of the translator's ideas. The moral is that whenever possible translation should be done cooperatively by translator and subject specialist. Translators may be located through the ASLIB *Register of specialist translators.* Recent Russian scientific technical and medical articles of general interest may be translated free of charge by NLL for organisations which agree to edit the draft translation.

PERSONAL REFERENCE FILES

Every psychologist, whether academic or practical, soon develops a collection of references to the literature and other material which he considers to be worth saving. The information to be recorded was discussed on page 59. This section is concerned with the storage and retrieval of the information. As the collection grows so too does the problem of retrieving information from it. At the outset a simple system filed alphabetically by author, or a simple subject classification is likely to be adequate. Problems begin to arise when the author's name is forgotten, or each of the subject classes becomes large, necessitating a tedious search for each reference. At this point either the collection is ignored or some more appropriate system developed. Two popular methods are edge punched cards and coordinate indexing.

Edge punched cards, often called 'Cope-Chat' cards, an abbreviation of Copeland-Chatterson, one of the major suppliers, are available in several sizes with holes around all or some of their edges. Information can be recorded on the body of the card, and relevant holes opened by a special punch leaving a v-shaped notch at the edge of the card. Information is retrieved by passing a needle through the pack of cards at the appropriate hole position and shaking the pack, allowing those cards which have been notched to fall. Several sortings will be necessary to obtain references which combine several characteristics, the cards thus being notched at several positions. As information will generally be retrieved by author or subject, sometimes by date, or type of document, each card must be coded under these headings. Direct coding, with one hole representing one category, will soon be found to be insufficient, as a 6 by 4 inch card will only have some seventy five holes. Various systems of indirect coding are used, with multiple punching of a group of holes ('field'); details are given in Foskett, A C A guide to personal indexes, second edition, 1970, Clive Bingley and Archon Books. In these systems coding and retrieval are complex operations and this can be time consuming and tedious with a large reference file.

Co-ordinate indexing appears more elaborate and the equipment is likely to cost more than with edge punched cards, but searching and retrieval are easier and may be done in more detail, and filing is a relatively unskilled job which can be done by a clerical assistant. Each reference is written on a separate card, which is given a serial number (accession number) and the cards are filed in this order. References are classified by underlining the key words, which are also known as 'descriptors' and 'uniterms', in the reference and abstract; and if an appropriate word does not appear it can be added. The number of words identified will vary according to the judged importance of the document, but will generally vary between 6 and 15.

Consistency in the selection of appropriate key words can be achieved by the development of a personal thesaurus showing links between related, superordinate and subordinate terms. The thesaurus can be generated by analysing an existing reference file, or developed from a subject index such as *Psychological abstracts* or *Medical subject headings* (*MeSH*) bearing in mind one's particular interests. Once developed, the thesaurus will be useful in analysing problems prior to searching (*see* chapter 5). Some key words may become overloaded as one's interests develop and this will reduce the efficiency of the system as too many reference cards will be thrown up when using that particular key word. It will then be necessary to subdivide the key word into its more specific components.

A second set of cards is established with one card for each key word, and the serial numbers of all references classified using this key word are entered on the keyword card. When information is required on a specific topic, then the appropriate keyword card is consulted and all references whose numbers appear there can be retrieved. More frequently a detailed retrieval of information classified under more than one key word will be needed. In these cases the numbers common to two or more keyword cards can be retrieved. Thus the search can be as fine as desired, for if too many references are located, a further relevant key word can be used to limit the search.

If key words are underlined as documents are first seen, then the classification of references by posting the accession number on to the appropriate keyword cards is a simple routine. The keyword cards can be simple index cards ruled to accommodate accession numbers, Broadhurst (*American psychologist*, 1962 17 (4)), pages 137-142) gives details of such a system in operation. Punched cards can also be used and coincidence of holes used to indicate common documents. The latter systems are also known as optical coincidence, or peek-a-boo systems; details can be found in Foskett (*op cit*) and Shackel *Human factors*, 1965 7 (5), pages 431-449. A computer based personal reference file could be established using the coordinate indexing principles. An advantage of coordinate indexing is that it can be used for material in addition to the reference file. Its advocates use it for personal papers, correspondence, research ideas files, press cuttings, slides and other visual aids.

APPENDIX A

ASSOCIATIONS AND SOCIETIES CONNECTED WITH PSYCHOLOGY

INTERNATIONAL

Congrès de Psychanalystes de langues romanes (Dr Pierre Luquet), 187, rue Saint-Jacques, Paris 5e.

Experimental Psychology and Animal Behaviour Section, International Union of Biological Sciences (Prof F A Stafleu), Botanisch Museum, Lange Niewstraat 106, Utrecht, Netherlands.

Fedération européenne de psychanalyse (Dr Raymond de Saussure), 2 rue Tertasse, Geneva.

Interamerican Society of Psychology (SIP), 1801 Lavaca Street 11-E, Austin, Texas 78701, USA.

International Association for Analytical Psychology, Gemeindestrasse 27, 8032 Zürich, Switzerland.

International Association of Applied Psychology (IAAP) (Prof G Westerlund), Sveavägen 65, Stockholm Va.

International Association of Individual Psychology (IAIP) (Dr Knut Baumgartel), Tuchlaben 7/9, 1010 Vienna.

International Ergonomics Association (IEA) (Prof E Grandjean), Institut für Hygiene und Arbeitsphysiologie, Eidgenössischen Technische Hochschule, Clausiusstrasse 25, 8006 Zurich, Switzerland.

International Psycho-analytical Association (Dr M M Montessori), 2B Prins Hendriklaan, Amsterdam z.

International Society for Normal and Abnormal Ethnopsychology (Dr C Pidoux), 96 rue Pierre Demeurs, Paris 17e.

International Society for the Psychology of Writing (ISPW), Corso XXII Marzo 57, 20129 Milan, Italy.

International Union of Scientific Psychology (Prof Eugene H Jacobsen), Dept of Psychology, Michigan State University, East Lansing, Michigan 48823, USA.

Société de psychologie médicale de langue français (P H Davost), 2 rue de Rohan, 35 Rennes, France.

Western European Association for Aviation Psychology (F J Miret y Alsina), 35 rue Cardinal Mercier, Brussels 1.

World Federation for Mental Health (WFMH), 1 rue Gevray, 1201 Geneva.

World Psychiatric Association (Dr Denys Leigh), Maudlsey Hospital, Denmark Hill, London SE 5.

Adlerian Society of Great Britain, c/o 4 Crediton Hill, Hampstead, London NW 6.

Association for Child Psychology and Psychiatry, c/o Adam House, 1 Fitzroy Square, London WIP 5AH.

Association of Child Psychotherapists, c/o Burgh House, New End Square, London NW 3.

Association of Educational Psychologists, c/o 3 Grange Court, Heworth, Felling, Gateshead, Co Durham.

Association for Humanistic Psychology, 17 Hanover Square, London WIR OEB.

Association for Programmed Learning, 27 Torrington Square, London WCI.

Association of Psychotherapists and the Society of Psychotherapy, c/o 411 Upper Richmond Road, London SW 15.

Association for Research in Infant and Child Development, c/o 4 North Drive, Great Baddow, Essex.

Association of Teachers of Psychology, c/o 18-19 Albemarle Street, London WIX 4DN.

British Psycho-Analytical Society, 63 New Cavendish Street, London WI.

British Psychological Society, 18-19 Albemarle Street, London WIX 4DN.

Centre for the Analytic Study of Student Problems, 26 Montague Square, London WI.

Ergonomics Research Society, c/o R G Sell, Construction Industry Training Board, Radnor House, London Road, Norbury, London SW 16.

Experimental Psychology Society, c/o Dr David Legge, Department of Psychology, Sir John Cass School of Science and Technology, Central House Annexe, Whitechapel High Street, London EI 7PF.

Group Analytic Practice, 88 Montague Mansions, London WI.

Guild of Pastoral Psychology, c/o 25 Porchester Terrace, London W2.

Hampstead Clinic, 21 Maresfield Gardens, London SW 3.

Independent Assessment and Research Centre Ltd, 57 Marylebone High Street, London WIM 3AE.

Institute of Child Psychology. 6 Pembridge Villas, London W11.

National Association for Mental Health, 39 Queen Anne Street, London W1.

National Bureau for Co-operation in Child Care, Adam House, 1 Fitzroy Square, London W1.

National Foundation for Educational Research, The Mere, Upton Park, Slough, Bucks.

National Institute of Industrial Psychology, 14 Welbeck Street, London W1.

Royal Medico-Psychological Association, Chandos House, 2 Queen Anne Street, London W1.

Scottish Council for Research in Education, 46 Moray Place, Edinburgh.

Society of Analytical Psychology, 30 Devonshire Place, London W1.

Society for Psychical Research, 1 Adam and Eve Mews, London W8.

Society for Research into Higher Education, 2 Woburn Square, London WC 1.

APPENDIX B

SOME PRIMARY JOURNALS IN PSYCHOLOGY

For further details *see:* Tompkins, M and Shirley, N *A checklist of serials in psychology and allied fields,* Troy, New York; Whitston Publishing Co, 1969 261 pages. Details of new journals are given in *Social science information.*

Key to Contents:

G General and Comprehensive
R Statistical, mathematical, research techniques
D Differential
P Physiological, comparative
L Learning and Thinking

M Motivation and Emotion
S Social
A Abnormal and Clinical
E Developmental and Educational
I Industrial and Occupational

	G	R	L	P	A	E	I
Acta psychologica: (European)	G						
American journal of mental deficiency					A		
American journal of psychology	G						
American journal of psychotherapy					A		
American psychologist	G						
Animal behaviour				P			
L'annee psychologique	G						
Annual of animal psychology (Japan)				P			
Archiv für die gesamte psychologie (Germany*	G						
Archives de psychologie (Switzerland)	G						
Arquivos Brasileiros de psicologia aplicada					A	E	I
Australian journal of psychology	G						
Australian psychologist	G						
Behaviour research methods and instrumentation		R					
Behavioral science	G	R					
Behaviour research and therapy			L		A		

94

Behavior therapy			L		A	
BINOP—*Bulletin de l'Institut National d'Etude du Travail et d'Orientation professionelle* (France)						E	I
Bollettino di psicologia applicata (Italy)				S			I
British journal of educational psychology						E	
British journal of mathematical and statistical psychology	R						
British journal of medical psychology					A		
British journal of psychology	G						
British journal of social and clinical psychology				S	A		
Bulletin de psychologie scolaire et d'orientation (Belgium)		D				E	
Cahiers de psychologie (France)		P					I
Canadian journal of psychology	G						
Canadian psychologist	G						
Caracterologie (France)		D					
Československá psychologie (Czechoslovakia)	G						
Child development						E	
Clinical psychologist					A		
Comparative group studies				S			
Conditional reflex			L		A		
Developmental psychology						E	
Educational and psychological measurement		D					
Ergonomics							I
Exceptional children						E	
Group psychotherapy				S	A		
Human inquiries: review of existential psychology and psychiatry	G				A		
Human factors							I
Human relations				S			
Indian journal of applied psychology						E	I
Indian journal of psychology	G						
Information psychologique (Belgium)						E	I
InterAmerican journal of psychology	G						

Journal	G	D	P	L	S	A	E	I
International journal of group psychotherapy					S	A		
International journal of man-machine studies								I
International journal of psychology	G							
International review of applied psychology							E	I
Japanese annals of social psychology					S			
Japanese journal of clinical psychology (Richo shinrigaku)						A		
Japanese journal of educational psychology							E	
Japanese journal of psychology (Shinrigaku kenkyu)	G							
Japanese psychological review (Shinrigaku hyoron)	G							
Journal de psychologie normale et pathologique (France)	G					A		
Journal of abnormal psychology						A		
Journal of applied behavioral science							E	I
Journal of applied psychology								I
Journal of biosocial science		D	P		S			
Journal of child psychology and psychiatry and allied disciplines							E	
Journal of clinical psychology		D				A		
Journal of comparative physiological psychology			P					
Journal of consulting and clinical psychology		D				A		
Journal of counseling psychology						A	E	I
Journal of creative behavior				L			E	
Journal of cross cultural psychology					S			
Journal of educational measurement		D					E	
Journal of educational psychology							E	
Journal of experimental child psychology							E	
Journal of the experimental analysis of behaviour			P	L				
Journal of experimental psychology	G							

	G	D	R	P	L	M	S	A	E	I
Journal of experimental research in personality		D								
Journal of experimental social psychology							S			
Journal of general psychology	G									
Journal of genetic psychology	G									
Journal of humanistic psychology		D				M				
Journal of individual psychology	G									
Journal of industrial psychology										I
Journal of mathematical psychology			R							
Journal of mental science								A		
Journal of motor behavior				P						
Journal of personality		D								
Journal of personality and social psychology		D					S			
Journal of projective techniques and personality assessment		D								
Journal of psychological researches (India)	G									
Journal of psychological studies	G									
Journal of psychology	G									
Journal of psychology (Shinri kenkyu) (Japan)	G									
Journal of psychopharmacology				P				A		
Journal of school psychology									E	
Journal of social issues	G						S			
Journal of social psychology							S			
Journal of verbal learning and verbal behaviour				P	L					
Kölner zeitschrift für soziologie und sozialpsychologie (Germany)							S			
Language and speech				P	L					
Learning and motivation					L	M				
Magyar pszichológia szemle (Hungary)	G									
Manpower and applied psychology										I
Merrill-Palmer quarterly of behavior and development		D					S		E	
Mind	G									
Multivariate behavior research							S			

Nederlands Tijdschrift voor de psychologie en haar grensgebieden	G				
Neuropsychologia		P			
Nordisk psykologi (Denmark)	G				
Occupational psychology					I
Organizational behavior and human performance					I
Perception and psychophysics		P			
Perceptual and motor skills		P			
Personnel and guidance journal				A	I
Personnel psychology					I
Physiology and behavior		P			
Professional psychology	G				
Przeglad psychologiczny (Poland)	G				
Psychologica Belgica	G				
Psychological bulletin	G				
Psychological record	G				
Psychological reports	G				
Psychological review			R		
Psychological studies (India)	G				
Psychologie Française	G				
Psychologie und praxis (Germany)				A	I
Psychologische beitrage (Germany)	G				
Psychologische forschung (Germany)	G				
Psychologische Rundschau (Germany)	G				
Psychometrika			R		
Psychonomic science		P L			
Psychopharamacologia (Germany)		P		A	
Psychophysiology		P			
Pszichologiai tanulmanyok (Hungary)	G				
Quarterly journal of experimental psychology		P L			
Revista Latinoamericana de psicologia	G				
Revista Mexicana de psicologia	G				
Revista de psicologia general y aplicada (Spain)	G	D		S	
Revista di psicologia (Italy)	G				

Journal	G	D	S	A	E	I	P
Revista de psicologia normal e patologica (Brazil)	G			A			
Revista di psicologia sociale e archivio Italiano de psicologia generale e del lavoro	G		S			I	
Revista de psihologie (Rumania)	G				E	I	
Revue internationale d'ethnopsychologie	G		S				
Revue de psychologie appliquée (France)		D				I	
Revue de psychologie et de pedagogie (Belgium)					E		
Revue Roumaine des sciences sociales serie de psychologie (Rumania)	G					I	
Revue Suisse de psychologie pure et appliquée (Switzerland)	G						
Scandinavian journal of psychology	G						
Sociometry			S				
Studia psychologica (Czechoslovakia)	G						
Travail human (France)						I	
Vita humana (Switzerland)					E		
Voprosy psihologii (USSR)	G						
Zeitschrift für experimentelle und angewandte psychologie (Germany)	G		S		E		
Zeitschrift für psychologie (Germany)	G						
Zeitschrift für psychotherapie und medizinische psychologie (Germany)	G			A			
Zeitschrift für sozial psychologie (Germany)			S				
Zeitschrift für tierpsychologie (Germany)							P

APPENDIX C

Chinese sociology and anthropology
Foreign psychiatry
International journal of mental health
International journal of sociology

Japanese psychological research
Psychologia
Soviet neurology and psychiatry
Soviet psychology
Soviet sociology

APPENDIX D

NEWSLETTERS, HOUSE JOURNALS, ETC

AAAS bulletin. American Association for the Advancement of Science, 1515 Massachusetts Avenue NW, Washington DC, USA.

AAPCC newsletter. American Association of Psychiatric Clinics for Children, 250 West 57th Street, New York 19, USA.

ACLS newsletter. American Council of Learned Societies, 345 East 46th Street, New York, USA.

ACPA newsletter. American Catholic Psychological Association, Fordham University, Bronx, New York 10458, USA.

Adding life to years. Institute of Gerontology, University of Iowa, 6 Byington Road, Iowa City, Iowa, USA.

AEGC newsletter. Association of Educators of Gifted Children, Admin Annex, 224 French Street, Erie, Pennsylvania, USA.

AIM technical interface. AIM Associates Cambridge Ltd, Bar Hill, Cambridge, CB3 8EZ.

ASAP calendar—newsletter. American Society of Adlerian Psychology, West Virginia University, Morgantown, West Virginia 26506, USA.

BACIE news. British Association for Commercial and Industrial Education, 16 Park Crescent, London WIN 4AP.

Behavioural technology. Electronics Centre, University of Essex, Colchester.

Bio-medical electronics. Industry Reports Incorporated, 514 10th Street NW, Washington DC 20004, USA.

British universities film council newsletter. 72 Dean Street, London WIV 5HB.

CRCR newsletter. Center for Rate Controlled Recordings, University of Louisville, Louisville, Kentucky 40208, USA.

Cross cultural social psychology newsletter. Dept of Political Science, Gakushuin (Peers') University, Mejiro Toshima-Ku, Tokyo, Japan.

Correctional psychologist. American Association of Correctional Psychologists, Box B, Anamosa, Iowa, USA.

Dawe digest. Dawe Instruments Ltd, Concord Road, Western Avenue, London W3.

ERB newsletter. Educational Records Bureau, 21 Audubon Avenue, New York, USA.

ERS news. (The newsletter of the Ergonomics Research Society). Ergonomics Laboratory, EMI Electronics Ltd, Feltham, Middlesex.

Farnell news. Farnell Instruments Ltd, Sandbeck Way, Wetherby, LS22 4DH.

Feelings and their medical significance. Ross Laboratories, Columbus, Ohio, USA.

FRNM bulletin (formerly *Parapsychological bulletin*). College Station, Durham, N Carolina 27708, USA.

Foundation news. Foundation Library Centre, 428 East Preston Street, Baltimore 2, Maryland, USA.

Foundation for research of human behavior—newsletter. 508 East William Street, Ann Arbor, Michigan, USA.

Hearing and speech news. National Association of Hearing and Speech Agencies, 919 18th Street NW, Washington DC 20006, USA.

Human relations training news. NTL Institute for Applied Behavioral Science, 1201 16th Street NW, Washington DC 20036, USA.

ICVA news. International Council of Voluntary Agencies, Avenue de la Paix 7, Geneva.

Individual psychology newsletter. International Association of Individual Psychology, 6 Vale Rise, London NW11.

Industrial and scientific instruments. Hanover Press Ltd, 4 Mill Street, London W1.

International mental health research newsletter. 124 East 28th Street, New York 10016, USA.

Interbehavioral psychology newsletter ('development and dissemination of objective approaches to psychology '). Noel W Smith, Faculty of Social Sciences, State University of Arts and Sciences, Plattsburgh, New York 12901, USA.

ISR newsletter. Institute for Social Research, The University of Michigan, Ann Arbor, Michigan 48106, USA.

Journal and newsletter (of the Association of Educational Psychologists). Circulation manager—R S Reid Esq, 94 Chatsworth Road, Croydon, Surrey.

The laboratory primate newsletter. Psychology Primate Laboratory, Brown University, Providence, Rhode Island 02912, USA.

Market Research Society newsletter. Market Research Society, 39 Hertford Street, London WIY 8EP.

Newsletter of the Parapsychology Foundation. 29 West 57th Street, New York 10019, USA.

New technology. Ministry of Technology, 42 Parliament Street, London SWI.

News bulletin. NFER Publishing Co Ltd, 2 Jennings Yard, Thames Avenue, Windsor. SI4 IQS.

Newsletter of history of psychology. Department of Psychology, University of Akron, Akron, Ohio 44304.

Newsletter on newsletters. The Newsletter Clearinghouse, 20 North Wacker Drive, Chicago, Illinois 60606, USA.

Newsletter for research in psychology. Veterans Administration Centre, Bay Pines, Florida 33504, USA.

Psychiatric news. American Psychiatric Association, 1700 18th Street NW, Washington 9 DC, USA.

Psychopharmacology bulletin. Psychopharmacology Research Branch, National Institute of Mental Health, 5454 Wisconsin Avenue, Chevy Chase, Maryland 20015, USA.

Programmed learning news. Association for Programmed Learning and Educational Technology, 27 Torrington Square, London WCI.

Registered criminologists' newsletter. American Association of Criminology, 141 First Parish Road, Scituate Harbor, Massachusetts, USA.

Reports on education. Department of Education and Science, Curzon Street, London WI.

Report on questionnaires. American Council on Education, 1 Dupont Circle, Washington DC 20036, USA.

SIP newsletter. Interamerican Society of Psychology, 1801 Lavaca Street 11-E, Austin, Texas 78701, USA.

SK and F psychiatric reporter. Smith Kline and French Laboratories, 1500 Spring Garden Street, Philadelphia 19101, USA.

Social Science Research Council newsletter. Social Science Research Council, State House, High Holborn, London WCI.

Social Science Research Council data bank newsletter. University of Essex, Colchester, Essex.

Teaching of psychology in schools. Dr John Radford, Dept of Psychology, West Ham College of Technology, Stratford, London EI5.

Transcultural psychiatric research review and newsletter. 1025 Pine Avenue West, Montreal, Canada.

University equipment. Benn Bros Ltd, 18/19 Whitefriars Street, London EC4Y 8BT.

Unscheduled events. Disaster Research Centre, Dept of Sociology, Ohio State University, Columbus, Ohio 43201, USA.

The Washington report. American Psychological Association, 1200 17th Street, Washington DC 20036, USA.

APPENDIX E

Index to BOOK REVIEWS in the humanities.

BUSINESS periodicals index.

CHILD development abstracts
and bibliography.

British Psychological Society:
(Educational, CHILD and clinical psychology) abstracts.

Exceptional CHILD education abstracts.

Science CITATION index.

British Psychological Society
(Educational, child and CLINICAL psychology) abstracts.

Perceptual COGNITIVE development.

Communications in behavioral
biology: part B (COMPARATIVE psychology).

Internationale Bibliographie der
Zeitschriftenliteratur (COMPREHENSIVE index covering all fields of knowledge).

COMPUTER abstracts.

COMPUTER and information
systems (abstracts).

COMPUTER program abstracts.

(British) national COMPUTER program index.

Cumulative COMPUTER abstracts.

East European scientific abstracts:
cybernetics COMPUTERS and automation.

USSR scientific abstracts: cybernetics COMPUTERS and automation.

COMPUTING reviews.

Current index to CONFERENCE papers in life
sciences.

Directory of published proceedings (CONFERENCE).

Index of CONFERENCE proceedings received by the NLL.

Proceedings in print (index to CONFERENCE proceedings).

World list of future international
meetings (CONFERENCES).

Novinky literatury—spolecenske
vedy—rada VII (Czechoslovakia— EDUCATION).
Research in EDUCATION.
Research into higher EDUCATION abstracts.
Technical EDUCATION abstracts.
British Psychological Society (EDUCATIONAL, child and clinical psychology) abstracts.
EMPLOYMENT relations abstracts.
ERGONOMICS abstracts.
EXCEPTIONAL child education abstracts.
Abstracts of FOLKLORE studies.
Readers' guide to periodical literature (GENERAL MAGAZINES).
Adult development and aging abstracts (GERONTOLOGY).
Excerpta medica : section 20 GERONTOLOGY and geriatrics.
Journal of GERONTOLOGY.
DSH abstracts (deafness, speech and HEARING).
PHRA : poverty and HUMAN RESOURCES abstracts.
British HUMANITIES index.
Indice general de publicaciones
periodicas Latinoamericanas (HUMANITIES and social sciences).
Index to book reviews in the HUMANITIES.
Social science and HUMANITIES index.
Excerpta medica : section 27 biophysics
bioengineering and medical INSTRUMENTATION.
Bulletin signaletique : 524 sciences du LANGAGE.
LANGUAGE and language behavior abstracts.
Bibliographie, programmierter
Unterricht (programmed LEARNING).
Current index to conference papers in LIFE SCIENCES.
MARKET RESEARCH abstracts.
Industrial MARKETING RESEARCH abstracts.
MATHEMATICAL reviews.
Aerospace MEDICINE and biology.

Index medicus (MEDICINE).

(MEETINGS *see* Conferences).

MENTAL HEALTH book review index.

Excerpta medica: section 8A NEUROLOGY and neurosurgery.

International abstracts in OPERATIONS RESEARCH.

OPHTHALMIC literature.

Excerpta medica: section 12 OPHTHALMOLOGY.

Vertical file index (PAMPHLETS).

PERCEPTUAL cognitive development.

PERSONNEL MANAGEMENT abstracts.

The PHILOSOPHER'S index.

Bibliographie de la PHILOSOPHIE.

Bulletin signaletique: 519 PHILOSOPHIE.

Repertoire bibliographique de la PHILOSOPHIE.

Abstract of Bulgarian scientific literature PHILOSOPHY and pedagogics.

Bulletin de informare stiintifica—(Rumania—PHILOSOPHY, logic, sociology, psychology).

Behavior and PHYSIOLOGY index (physiological psychology).

Selected RAND abstracts (PLANNING).

POPULATION index.

POPULATION and reproduction research abstracts.

PHRA: POVERTY and human resources abstracts.

Bibliographie, programmierter Unterricht (PROGRAMMED learning).

Excerpta medica: section 8B PSYCHIATRY.

PSYCHOLOGICAL abstracts.

Bulletin signaletique: 390 PSYCHOLOGIE, psychopathlogie.

L'annee PSYCHOLOGIQUE.

Behavior and physiology index
(physiological PSYCHOLOGY).
British Psychological Society
(Educational, child and clinical PSYCHOLOGY) abstracts.
Bulletin de informare stiintifica—
(Rumania—philosophy, logic, sociology PSYCHOLOGY).
Communications in behavioral biology:
part B (comparative PSYCHOLOGY).
International aerospace abstracts (PSYCHOLOGY as bioscience
and biotechnology).
Novinky literatury—spolecenske
vedy—rada IX—(Czechoslovakia PSYCHOLOGY).
STAR: scientific and technical
aerospace reports (PSYCHOLOGY as bioscience
and biotechnology).
PSYCHOPHARMACOLOGY abstracts.
PUBLIC AFFAIRS information
service bulletin.
Australian PUBLIC AFFAIRS information
service bulletin.
RACE RELATIONS abstracts.
REHABILITATION literature.
Excerpta medica: section 19 REHABILITATION and physical
medicine.
NLL announcements bulletin
(translations, REPORTS and theses).
STAR: scientific and technical
aerospace REPORTS.
US Government research and
development REPORTS.
Population and REPRODUCTION research abstracts.
Mental RETARDATION abstracts.
Index medicus (includes bibliography
of medical REVIEWS).
SCIENCE citation index.
SOCIAL SCIENCE and humanities index.

CIRF abstracts (vocational TRAINING).

TRANSLATIONS register index.

Commonwealth index to unpublished TRANSLATIONS (ASLIB).

Index translationum (TRANSLATIONS).

NLL announcements bulletin (TRANSLATIONS, reports and theses).

ETC world index of scientific TRANSLATIONS.

APPENDIX F

Advances in child DEVELOPMENT and behavior.
Annual progress in child psychiatry and
child DEVELOPMENT.
Bibliotheca vita humana (human DEVELOPMENT).
Review of EDUCATIONAL research.
Advances in GENETICS.
Annual review of GENETICS.
Advances in bioengineering and INSTRUMENTATION.
The psychology of LEARNING and motivation.
Advances in MATHEMATICS.
Progress in MATHEMATICS.
Progress in community MENTAL HEALTH.
Yearbook of psychiatry and applied MENTAL HEALTH.
Sociological METHODOLOGY.
Nebraska symposium on MOTIVATION.
The psychology of learning and MOTIVATION.
International review of NEUROBIOLOGY.
Progress in NEUROBIOLOGY.
Progress in NEUROLOGY and psychiatry.
Yearbook of NEUROLOGY and neurosur-
gery.
Progress in OPERATIONS RESEARCH.
Survey of OPHTHALMOLOGY.
Yearbook of OPHTHALMOLOGY.
Progress in experimental PERSONALITY research.
PHARMACOLOGICAL reviews.
Advances in PHARMACOLOGY and chemo-
therapy.
Annual review of PHARMACOLOGY.
PHILOSOPHICAL books (book
reviews).
PHYSIOLOGICAL reviews.
Progress in PHYSIOLOGICAL psychology.
Annual review of PHYSIOLOGY.
Contributions to sensory PHYSIOLOGY.
Annual review in automatic PROGRAMMING (computers).
Current PSYCHIATRIC therapies.

Bibliotheca PSYCHIATRICA.

PSYCHIATRY and social science
review (book reviews).

Annual progress in child PSYCHIATRY and child development.

Modern perspectives in international
child PSYCHIATRY.

Progress in neurology and PSYCHIATRY.

Recent advances in biological PSYCHIATRY.

Yearbook of PSYCHIATRY and applied
mental health.

International journal of PSYCHOANALYSIS.

PSYCHOLOGICAL bulletin.

Advances in PSYCHOLOGICAL assessment.

Jahrbuch für PSYCHOLOGIE Psychotherapie
und medizinische anthropo-
logie.

L'annee PSYCHOLOGIQUE.

Advances in experimental social PSYCHOLOGY.

Advances in the study of behavior
(comparative PSYCHOLOGY).

Annual review of PSYCHOLOGY.

Bibliotheca primatologica (comparative PSYCHOLOGY).

Contemporary PSYCHOLOGY (book reviews).

Current topics in clinical and community PSYCHOLOGY.

Minnesota symposium on child PSYCHOLOGY.

Progress in clinical PSYCHOLOGY.

Progress in physiological PSYCHOLOGY.

The PSYCHOLOGY of learning and
motivation.

Advances in biochemical PSYCHOPHARMACOLOGY.

Advances in PSYCHOSOMATIC medicine.

Jahrbuch für Psychologie PSYCHOTHERAPIE und medizinische Anthropologie.

International review of research in
mental RETARDATION.

Contributions to SENSORY physiology.

Advances in experimental SOCIAL psychology.

Current topics and clinical and community psychology (SOCIAL).

Psychiatry and SOCIAL SCIENCE review (book reviews).

SOCIOLOGICAL methodology.

Current SOCIOLOGY.

Current psychiatric THERAPIES.

APPENDIX G

For more comprehensive details *see*: Harvard University: *The Harvard list of books in psychology* (third edition). Harvard University Press, 1965, 111 pages (a fourth edition is expected in 1971).

SECTION A: General reference (corresponds to sections I, II, and III of Harvard list).

Berelson, Bernard and Steiner, Gary A: *Human behavior: an inventory of scientific findings.* Harcourt, Brace and World, 1964, 712 pages.

Cattell, Raymond B: *Handbook of multivariate experimental psychology.* Rand McNally, 1967, 959 pages.

Ellis, Albert and Abarbanel, Albert: *The encyclopedia of sexual behavior* (two volumes). Hawthorn Books, 1967.

Gilbertson, G (translator): *Encyclopaedia of cybernetics* (translation of Muller, A (ed): *Lexikon der Kybernetic.* Hamburg Verlag Schnelle, 1964). Manchester University Press, 1968, 214 pages.

Metzger, Wolfgang and Erke, H: *Handbuch der Psychologie* (twelve volumes). Gottingen, Verlag für Psychologie: Hogrefe, 1966.

Neel, Ann F: *Theories of psychology: a handbook.* Cambridge (Massachusetts), Schenkman, 1969, 482 pages.

Sahakian, William S: *History of psychology: a source book in systematic psychology.* Itasca (Illinois), Peacock ,1968.

Sills, David L (ed): *International encyclopaedia of the social sciences* (seventeen volumes). New York; Macmillan & Free Press, 1968.

Koch, Sigmund: *Psychology: a study of a science* (six volumes). McGraw-Hill, 1959-63.

Osgood, Charles E: *Method and theory in experimental psychology.* Oxford University Press, 1953, 800 pages.

Stevens, S S (ed): *Handbook of experimental psychology.* Wiley, 1951, 1436 pages.

Woodworth, Robert S and Schlosberg, Harold: *Experimental psychology* (revised edition). Methuen, 1955, 948 pages.

SECTION B: Psychological statistics, Mathematical psychology, measurement and research techniques (corresponds to sections V and VI of Harvard list).

Abramowitz, M and Stegun, I A (eds): *Handbook of mathematical functions with formulas, graphs and mathematical tables*. Dover, 1965, 1046 pages.

Chakravarti, I M, Laha, R G and Roy, J: *Handbook of methods of applied statistics* (two volumes). Wiley, 1967.

Computer Consultants Ltd: *European computer user's handbook 1970/71* (eighth edition). Pergamon, 1970.

Fletcher, A, Miller, J C P, Rosenhead, L and Comrie, L J: *Index of mathematical tables* (second edition: two volumes). Blackwell Scientific Publications, 1962, 994 pages.

Greenwood, J A and Hartley, H O: *Guide to tables in mathematical statistics*. Princeton University Press, 1962, 1014 pages.

Luce, R D, Bush, Robert R and Galanter, Eugene (eds): *Handbook of mathematical psychology* (three volumes). Wiley, 1963, 1965.

Markus, John: *Handbook of electronic control circuits*. McGraw-Hill, 1959.

Miller, Delbert C: *Handbook of research design and social measurement*. McKay Social Science Series, 1964, 332 pages.

Pfanzagl, J: *Theory of measurement*. Wiley, 1968.

Walsh, John E: *Handbook of nonparametric statistics* (three volumes). Van Nostrand, 1962, 1965, 1968.

Whitla, Dean K: *Handbook of measurement and assessment in behavioral sciences*. Addison-Wesley, 1968, 508 pages.

SECTION C: Psychological tests and individual differences including personality (corresponds to sections VII and XIX of Harvard list).

Borgatta, E F and Lambert, W W: *Handbook of personality theory and research*. Rand McNally, 1968, 1232 pages.

Buros, Oscar K: *Mental measurements yearbook* (third to seventh editions). Gryphon, 1949, 1953, 1959, 1965, 1971.

Cattell, R B and Warburton, F W: *Objective personality and motivation tests*. University of Illinois Press, 1967, 678 pages.

Cattell, R B (ed): *Handbook of modern personality theory*. Aldine, 1970.

Murstein, Bernard I: *Handbook of projective techniques*. Basic, 1965, 934 pages.

SECTION D: Physiological and comparative psychology (corresponds to sections VIII, IX, XXI and XII of Harvard list).

Blinkov, Samuil M and Glezer, Il'ya I: *The human brain in figures and tables: a quantitative handbook* (translated from Russian by Basil Haigh). Basic Books and Plenum Press, 1968.

Brown, C C: *Methods in psychophysiology.* Williams & Wilkins, 1967.

Damm, H C: *Handbook of clinical laboratory data.* Chemical Rubber Co, 1965, 469 pages.

Davson, Hugh (ed): *The eye* (four volumes). Academic Press, 1962.

Field, John, Magoun, H W and Hall, V E: *Handbook of physiology, section 1: neurophysiology* (three volumes). Washington, American Physiological Society, 1959-60.

Gray, Peter (ed): *Encyclopedia of the biological sciences.* Reinhold, 1961.

Hill, W C O: *Primates, comparative anatomy and taxonomy* (seven volumes). Wiley, 1953 et seq.

Hofer, H, Schultz, A H and Starck, D (eds): *Primatologia: Handbook of primatology.* Basel, Karger, 1956.

Howard, Ian P and Templeton, William B: *Human spatial orientation.* Wiley, 1966, 533 pages.

Kleitman, Nathaniel: *Sleep and wakefulness* (revised and enlarged edition). University of Chicago Press, 1963, 552 pages.

Moray, N: *Attention: selective processes in vision and hearing.* Hutchinson, 1970, 216 pages.

Otis, L and Bosley, J J: *Psychopharmacology handbook.* Bethesda, National Institutes of Health Psychopharmacology Service Center, 1960, 336 pages.

Venables, Peter H and Martin, Irene (eds): *A manual of psychophysiological methods.* Amsterdam, North Holland, 1967, 559 pages.

Vinken, P J and Bruyn, C W (eds): *Handbook of clinical neurology* (thirty volumes to be published). Wiley, 1968 et seq.

Wyszecki, Gunter and Stiles, W S: *Color science: concepts and methods, quantitative data and formulas,* Wiley, 1967, 628 pages.

SECTION E: Learning and thinking (corresponds to sections XIII, XIV, XV of Harvard list).

Abelson, Robert P and Aronson, Elliot (*et als,* eds): *Theories of cognitive consistency: a sourcebook.* Rand McNally, 1968, 901 pages.

Adams, J A: *Human memory.* McGraw-Hill, 1967, 326 pages.

Bilodeau, Edward A (ed): *Acquisition of skill.* Academic, 1966, 539 pages.

Cavanagh, Peter and Jones, Clive: *Yearbook of educational and institutional technology 1969/70 incorporating programmes in print.* Cornmarket Press, 1969, 459 pages.

Kimble, Gregory A: *Hilgard and Marquis' conditioning and learning* (second edition). Methuen, 1961, 590 pages.

Leith, George O M (with the assistance of Peel, E A and Curr, W): *A handbook of programmed learning* (second edition). Birmingham, 1966, 152 pages.

Lysaught, Jerome P and Williams, Clarence M: *A guide to programmed instruction.* Wiley, 1963.

Osgood, C E and Sebeok, T A (eds): *Psycholinguistics: a survey of theory and research problems.* Indiana University Press, 1965.

SECTION F: Motivation and emotion (corresponds to sections XVI, XVII of Harvard list).

Arnold, Magda B: *Emotion and personality* (two volumes). Cassell, 1961.

Arnold, Magda B (ed): *Feelings and emotions.* Academic Press, 1970.

Cofer, Charles N. and Appley, Mortimer H: *Motivation: theory and research.* Wiley, 1964, 958 pages.

Madsen, K B: *Theories of motivation* (fourth edition). Ohio, Kent State University Press, 1968, 365 pages.

Young, Paul T: *Motivation and emotion: a survey of determinants of human and animal activity.* Wiley, 1961.

SECTION G: Social psychology (corresponds to sections XX, XXI, XXII of Harvard list).

Bauer, Raymond A (ed): *Social indicators.* MIT Press, 1966, 357 pages.

Coleman, James S: *Introduction to mathematical sociology.* Free Press, 1964, 544 pages.

Faris, Robert E L: *Handbook of modern sociology.* Rand McNally, 1964, 1088 pages.

Goslin, David A (ed): *Handbook of socialization theory and research.* Rand McNally, 1969, 1182 pages.

Hare, Alexander P: *Handbook of small group research.* Collier-Macmillan, 1962, 512 pages.

Lindzey, G and Aronson, Elliot (eds): *Handbook of social psychology* (second edition; five volumes). Addison Wesley, 1968.

Wagner, R H and Arnold, C C: *Handbook of group discussion* (second edition). Houghton-Mifflin, 1965.

SECTION H: Abnormal psychology (corresponds to sections XXIII, XXIV of Harvard list).

Arieti, Silvano (ed): *American handbook of psychiatry* (three volumes). Basic Books, 1959, 1966.

Carter, Charles H: *Handbook of mental retardation syndromes.* Springfield (Illinois), Thomas, 1966, 168 pages.

Costello, Charles G (ed): *Symptoms of psychopathology: a handbook.* Wiley, 1970, 648 pages.

Eidelberg, Ludwig: *Encyclopedia of psychoanalysis* (two volumes). Collier-Macmillan, 1968, 571 pages.

Ellis, Norman R (ed): *Handbook of mental deficiency: psychological theory and research.* McGraw-Hill, 1963, 722 pages.

Eysenck, Hans J (ed): *Handbook of abnormal psychology: an experimental approach.* Pitman, 1960, 816 pages.

Freedman, Alfred M and Kaplan, Harold I (eds): *Comprehensive textbook of psychiatry* Williams and Wilkins, 1967, 1666 pages.

Gordon, Jesse E: *Handbook of clinical and experimental hypnosis.* Collier-Macmillan, 1967, 653 pages.

Grinstein, Alexander: *The index of psychoanalytic writings* (five volumes). New York, International University Press, 1956-60.

Laughlin, Henry P: *The neuroses* (with glossary of psychiatric concepts). Butterworth, 1967, 1076 pages.

Moreno, J L *et al* (eds): *The international handbook of group psychotherapy.* New York, Philosophical Library, 1966, 747 pages.

Quay, Herbert C (ed): *Juvenile delinquency: research and theory.* Van Nostrand, 1965, 350 pages.

Travis, Lee E (ed): *Handbook of speech pathology.* New York, Appleton-Century-Crofts, 1957, 1088 pages.

Wolman, Benjamin B (ed): *Handbook of clinical psychology.* McGraw-Hill, 1965, 1596 pages.

SECTION J: Developmental and educational psychology (corresponds to sections XXV, XXVI, of Harvard list).

Birren, J E: *The psychology of aging.* Prentice Hall, 1964, 303 pages.

Brackbill, Yvonne (ed): *Infancy and early childhood: a handbook and guide to human development.* Collier-Macmillan, 1967, 523 pages.

Falkner, F: *Human development.* Saunders, 1966.

Gottsegen, Monroe, and Gottsegen, Gloria B (eds): *Professional school psychology* (three volumes). Grune and Stratton, 1960-69.

Gruenberg, Sidonie M (ed): *The new encyclopedia of child care and guidance.* Doubleday, 1968.

Harris, Chester W (ed): *Encyclopedia of educational research* (third edition). New York, Macmillan, 1960.

Kirk, S A and Weiner, B B (eds): *Behavioral research on exceptional children.* Washington, Council for Exceptional Children, 1963, 2384 pages.

SECTION K: Industrial and organisational psychology (corresponds to sections XXVII, XXVIII of Harvard list).

Barber, J W (ed): *Industrial training handbook.* Iliffe, 1968, 402 pages.

Bennett, E, Degan, J and Spiegel, J: *Human factors in technology.* McGraw-Hill, 1963, 685 pages.

Blum, M and Naylor, J C: *Industrial psychology: its theoretical and social foundations* (revised edition). Harper, 1968, 633 pages.

Fogel, Lawrence J: *Biotechnology: concepts and applications.* Prentice Hall, 1963, 826 pages.

Fryer, D H and Henry, E R (eds): *Handbook of applied psychology* (two volumes). Holt Rinehart and Winston, 1950.

Guion, R M: *Personnel testing.* McGraw-Hill, 1965, 585 pages.

March, James G (ed): *Handbook of organizations.* Rand McNally, 1965, 1247 pages.

Morgan, Clifford T, Cook, Jesse S, Chapanis, Alphonse, and Lund, Max W (eds): *Human engineering guide to equipment design.* McGraw-Hill, 1963.

Tufts University, Institute for Applied Experimental Psychology: *Handbook of human engineering data* (second revised edition) Medford Massachusetts, Tufts University.

Vroom, V H: *Work and motivation.* Wiley, 1964, 331 pages.

Yoder, Dale, Heneman, H G, Turnbull, J G and Stone, C H: *Handbook of personnel management and labor relations.* McGraw-Hill, 1958.

APPENDIX H

To identify a foreign language *see*: Ostermann, Georg F von: *Manual of foreign languages* (fourth edition). New York, Central Book Co, 1952. Contains information about 130 languages and dialects; alphabet; pronunciation code; grammar; numbers, etc. Library and bibliographical terms and abbreviations for some languages.

For details of general foreign language dictionaries *see*: Collison, Robert L: *Dictionaries of foreign languages*. Haffner, 1955. Walford, A J: *A guide to foreign language grammars and dictionaries* (second edition). London, Library Association, 1967, 240 pages.

For details of foreign language dictionaries in subjects other than psychology use:

Marton, Tibor W: *Foreign language and English dictionaries in the physical sciences and engineering*. US Dept of Commerce, National Bureau of Standards, Miscellaneous Publication 258, 1964, 189 pages.

UNESCO: *Bibliography of interlingual scientific and technical dictionaries*. UNESCO, 1961. *Supplement to bibliography of interlingual scientific and technical dictionaries*. UNESCO, 1965.

PSYCHOLOGY AND RELATED SUBJECTS

Czech

Kujal, B: *Pedagogický slovník* (Educational dictionary). Prague, Státní pedagogické nakladatelství, 1967, 533 pages.

Danish

Nielsen, John B: *Psykiatrisk ordbog* (Psychiatric dictionary) (second edition). Kobenhavn, Host Sons Forlag, 1968, 138 pages.

French

Battro, Antonio M: *Dictionnaire d'Epistemologie génétique* (terms used in Piagetian research). Paris, Presses Univ de France, 1966, 188 pages.

Daco, P: *Guide de la psychologie moderne* (Psychology and psychoanalysis). Paris, Centre Nationale de Livre Familial, 1968, 516 pages.

Lafon, Robert: *Vocabulaire de psychopédagogie et de psychiatrie de l'enfant* (educational psychology and child psychiatry). Paris, Presses Univ de France, 1963, 604 pages.

Laplanche, Jean and Pontalis, J B: *Vocabulaire de la psychanalyse* (psychoanalysis). Paris, Presses Univ de France, 1968, 520 pages. *See also* Polyglot dictionaries.

Moor, Lise: *Glossaire de psychiatrie, de psychologie pathologique et de neuropsychiatrie infantile* (psychiatry, abnormal psychology and child neuro-psychiatry). Paris, Masson et Cie, 1966, 196 pages.

Piéron, H: Vocabulaire de la psychologie (psychology) (fourth edition). Paris, Presses Univ de France, 1968, 571 pages.

Porot, Antoine: *Manuel alphabetique de psychiatrie* (psychiatry) (third edition). Paris, Presses Univ de France, 1965, 584 pages.

Sillamy, Norbert: *Dictionnaire de la psychologie* (psychology). Paris, Editions Larousse, 1965, 319 pages.

German

Drever, James and Fröhlich, Werner, David: *DTV—Wörterbuch zur Psychologie* (psychology). München, Deutsche Taschenbuch Verlag, 1968, 303 pages.

Dorsch, Friedrich: *Psychologisches Wörterbuch* (psychology) (seventh edition). Bern, Huber, 1963, 552 pages.

Feldkeller, P: *Wörterbuch der Psychopolitik* (psychological terms used in politics, propaganda, leadership). Berne, Franke Verlag, 1967.

Haring, Claus and Leickert, Karl Heinz: *Wörterbuch der psychiatrie und ihrer Grenzgebiete* (psychiatry and related subjects). Stuttgart, F-K Schattauer Verlag, 1968, 634 pages.

Hehlmann, Wilhelm: *Wörterbuch der Psychologie* (psychology) (fourth edition). Stuttgart, Kröner, 1965, 684 pages.

Strachey, Alix: *A new German-English psychoanalytical vocabulary*. London, Bailliere, Tindall & Cox, 1943, 84 pages.

Sury, Kurt von: *Wörterbuch der Psychologie und ihrer Grenzgebiete* (psychology and related subjects) (third edition). Basel, Benno Schwabe & Co, 1967, 324 pages.

Polish

Pieter, J: *Slownik Psychologiczny* (psychological dictionary). Wroclaw, Ossolineum, 1963, 348 pages.

Ekel, J, Jaroszyński, J and Ostaszewska, J: *Maly slovnik psychologiczny* (Small psychological dictionary). Warszawa, Wiedza powszechna, 1965.

Russian

Kairov, I A: *Pedagogicheskii Slovar'* (Educational dictionary) (two volumes). Moscow, RSFSR Academy of Pedagogical Sciences, 1960.

Rozenman, A I: *Russko-Angliiskii Shkol' no-Pedagogicheskii Slovar'* (Russian-English educational dictionary). Yaroslav USSR, Yaroslav Publishing House, 1959, 455 pages.

Smith, R E F: *A Russian-English dictionary of social science terms.* London, Butterworth, 1962, 507 pages.

Telberg, Ina and Dmitrieff, A: *Russian-English glossary of psychiatric terms.* New York, Telberg Book Corporation, 1964, 86 pages.

Serbo-Croatian.

Frankovic, E, Pregrad, Z and Simlesa, P: *Enciklopedijski rjecnik pedagogije* (Encyclopedic dictionary of education). Zagreb, Matica Hrvatske, 1963, 1146 pages.

Hudolin, V: *Psihijatrijsko—psihološki leksikon* (Psychiatric and psychological dictionary). Zagreb, Privreda, 1963, 428 pages.

Polyglot

English, French, German

Duijker, Hubert C J: *Lexicon of Psychological Terms.* In preparation 1970.

English, German, Norwegian, Swedish

Havin, Henry: *Psykologisk Ordbok* (Psychological dictionary). Oslo, J C Tanum, 1950, 153 pages.

Czech, Russian, English, German

Brichaček, V, Hampejsová, O, Hoskovec, J and Štikar, J: Czech-Russian-English-German glossary of basic statistical terms used in psychology. Prague, Czechoslovak Psychological Society, 1960, 8 pages.

English, Czech, German

Hoskovec, J, Říčan, P and Mehl, J: *Významový slovniik základnich psychometrických terminů* (Glossary of psychometric terms). Prague, Czechoslovak Psychological Society, 1963, 19 pages.

German, English, Spanish, Italian, Portuguese

Laplanche, Jean and Pontalis, J B: *Vocabulaire de la Psychanalyse* (psychoanalysis). Paris, Presses Univ de France, 1968, 520 pages. Headings translated into German, English, Spanish, Italian and Portuguese.

Russian, English, French

Mikhailov, A I: *Russko-anglo-frantsuzskii terminologicheskii slovar' po informatsionnoi teorii i praktike* (Russian-English-French terminological dictionary on information theory and its practice). Moscow, Nauka, 1968, 240 pages.

APPENDIX I

American Psychiatric Association Committee on Public Information: *A psychiatric glossary: the meaning of words used frequently in psychiatry* (third edition). Springer, 1969, 80 pages.

Baldwin, J M: *Dictionary of Philosophy and Psychology* (three volumes). Macmillan, 1901-5 (reprinted in four volumes by Peter Smith).

Brussel, J A: *Dictionary of psychiatry*. Chambers, 1967, 234 pages.

Baker, R: *Dictionary of speech pathology*. Moore Publishing Co.

Catania, A Charles: *Contemporary research in operant behavior* (includes 23 page glossary). Scott, Foresman, 1968.

Chaplin, J P: *Dictionary of psychology*. New York, Dell Publications, 1968, 537 pages.

Drever, James A (revised edition by Wallerstein, Harvey): *A Dictionary of psychology*. Penguin, 1964, 320 pages.

English, Horace, Bidwell and English, Ava C: *A comprehensive dictionary of psychological and psychoanalytical terms*. Longmans, 1958, 594 pages.

Erdelyi, Michael and Grossman, Frank: *Dictionary of terms and expressions of industrial psychology*. New York, Pitman, 1939, 98 pages.

Fairchild, H F: *Dictionary of sociology*. Littlefield, 1944.

Ferm, Vergilius, T A: *A dictionary of pastoral psychology*. Owen, 1955, 336 pages.

Lewis, A: *Glossary of mental disorders* (*General Register Office*). HMSO, 1968, 32 pages.

Good, C V and Merkel, W R: *Dictionary of education* (second edition). McGraw-Hill, 1959.

Gould, Julius and Kolb, William L (eds): *Dictionary of the social sciences*. Tavistock, 1964, 761 pages.

Harriman, Philip L: *Handbook of psychological terms*. Paterson (New Jersey), Littlefield, Adams & Co, 1965, 222 pages.

Hinsie, Leland E and Campbell, Robert J: *Psychiatric Dictionary* (third edition). Oxford University Press, 1960, 788 pages.

Heidenreich, Charles A: *A dictionary of personality.* Dubuque (Iowa), William C Brown Co, 1968, 213 pages.

Heidenreich, Charles A: *A dictionary of general psychology: basic terminology and key concepts.* Dubuque (Iowa), Kendale/Hunt, 1970, 309 pages.

Hoult, Thomas F: *Dictionary of modern sociology.* Littlefield, 1969.

Laplanche, J and Pontalis, J B: *The language of psychoanalysis.* London, Hogarth Press, 1971.

Mitchell, G Duncan (ed): *A dictionary of sociology.* Routledge & Kegan Paul, 1968, 230 pages.

Moore, Burness E and Fine, Bernard D: *A glossary of psychoanalytic terms and concepts* (second edition). American Psychoanalytic Association, 1968, 102 pages.

Rosenthall and Yudkin (eds): *Dictionary of philosophy* (translated from Russian by Dixon, R R). Central Books, 494 pages.

Runes, D: *Dictionary of philosophy.* Owen, 343 pages.

Rycroft, Charles: *A critical dictionary of psychoanalysis.* Nelson, 1968, 189 pages.

Theodorson, George A and Theodorson, Achilles G: *A modern dictionary of sociology.* Methuen, 1970, 480 pages.

Verplanck, William S: *A glossary of some terms used in the objective science of behavior* (supplement to the *Psychological review,* 1957 64 (6) November, part 2). American Psychological Association, 42 pages.

Warren, Howard Crosby: *Dictionary of psychology.* Allen and Unwin, 1934, 372 pages.

Winick, C: *Dictionary of anthropology.* Littlefield, 1968.

Winn, Ralph B: *Dictionary of hypnosis.* Vision, 1965, 124 pages.

Zadrozny, J T: *Dictionary of social science.* Public Affairs Press, 1959.

APPENDIX J

(in subjects related to psychology)

GENERAL

For material on all subjects *see*:

1 Walford, A J: *Guide to reference material* (second edition), three vols. Library Association.

Vol 1: Science and technology, 1966.

Vol 2: Social and historical sciences, philosophy and religion, 1968.

Vol 3: Generalities, languages, the arts, literature, 1970.

2 Winchell, Constance M: *Guide to reference books* (eighth edition). American Library Association, 1968.

3 Sheehy, E P: *Supplement to guide to reference books*. American Library Association, 1968.

BIOLOGICAL SCIENCES (*see also* 11, 21)

4 Bottle, R T and Wyatt, H V: *The use of biological literature*. Butterworth and Archon Books, 1966 (second edition 1972).

5 Brunn, A L: *How to find out in pharmacy*. Pergamon, 1969.

6 Kerker, Ann E and Murphy, H T: *Biological and biomedical resource literature*. Purdue University, 1968.

7 Smith, Roger C and Painter, Reginald H: *Guide to the literature of the zoological sciences* (seventh edition). Burgess, 1966.

SOCIAL SCIENCES (*see also* 22, 23, 24)

8 White, C M: *Sources of information in the social sciences*. Bedminster, 1964.

9 Stevens, Roland E: *Reference books in the social sciences and humanities*. Illini Union Bookstore, 1966.

10 Borchardt, D H: *How to find out in philosophy and psychology*. Pergamon, 1968.

11 Albert, E M and Lasker, G: *Resources for the teaching of anthropology*. University of California Press, 1963.

12 Brock, C: *The literature of political science*. Bowker, 1969.

13 Wynar, L R: *Guide to reference materials in political science*, two vols. Libraries Unlimited, 1966/68.

14 Bristow, T and Holmes, B: *Comparative education through the literature*. Butterworth and Archon Books, 1968.

15 Foskett, D J: *How to find out: educational research*. Pergamon, 1965.

16 Manheim, T, Dardarian, G L and Satterthwaite, D A: *Sources in educational research*. Wayne State University Press, 1969.

17 Bakewell, K G B: *How to find out: management and productivity* (second edition). Pergamon, 1970.

18 Coman, E T: *Sources of business information* (second edition). University of California Press, 1964.

19 Maltby, A: *Economics and commerce: the sources of information and their organisation*. Clive Bingley and Archon Books, 1968.

20 Wills, Gordon: *Sources of UK marketing information*. Nelson, 1969.

21 Kelley, James G: *Community mental health and social psychiatry: a reference guide*. Harvard University Press, 1961.

PHYSICAL SCIENCES

22 Harvey, J M: *Sources of statistics*. Clive Bingley and Archon Books, 1969.

23 Wasserman, P: *Statistics sources* (second edition). Gale, 1965.

24 Buckland, W R and Fox, R A: *Bibliography of basic texts and monographs on statistical methods 1945-1960* (second edition). Oliver and Boyd, 1963.

25 Moore, C K and Spencer, K J: *Electronics: a bibliographical guide* (second edition). Macdonald, 1965.

26 Pritchard, Alan: *A guide to computer literature*. Clive Bingley and Archon Books, 1969.

5

INDEX

Psychology (*cont*)
teaching of 15, 92, 103
of writing 91
Psychometrics 14, 125 (*see also*
psychology: differential)
Psychopathology 121
Psychopharmacology 97, 98, 103,
110, 115, 119
Psychophysics 14, 98
Psychosomatics 115
Psychotherapy 92, 94, 99, 115, 116,
121
Public affairs 110
Publisher 79

Questionnaires 103

Race 110
Readings: collections of 48
Records (of literature search) 59,
60
Rehabilitation 110
Reliability 30
Report writing 70-71, 81-84
Reports 51-2, 110
Reproduction 110
Research intelligence 50, 52, 53, 73
(*see also* orientation)
Research in progress 50, 60, 67, 73
Research techniques 94, 118
Retardation 110, 115
Retrieval 60, 64, 68-9, 89
Reviews 37-8, 51, 54, 60, 110, 113
116
Rumania 99
Russia (*see* USSR)

Scattering 11, 13
Secondary interests 29
sources 33-34
Selective dissemination of informa-
tion 54, 55
Sexual behaviour 117

Skill 120 (*see also* motor behaviour)
Sleep 119
' Snowballing ' 67
Social security 111
Social work 13, 111
Sociology 13, 100, 111, 116, 120, 126,
127
Spain 98, 125
Spatial orientation 119
Speech 97, 102, 111, 121, 126
Standards 57 (*see also* British Stan-
dards, International Standards)
Statistics 14, 111, 118, 125, 129
Style manual 82
Supplementary publications scheme
83
Sweden 125
Switzerland 94, 99
Symposia 54

Technology 111, 122, 128
Tertiary sources 33-34
Tests (*see* psychology: differential)
Textbooks 48
Theories 117, 118, 119, 120, 121,
122
Thesaurus 49, 54, 56, 90
Theses 51, 107, 111
Thinking 94, 106, 119
Title 70, 82
Trade literature 36, 101-104
Training 102, 111, 122
Translation 86-88, 112
Transliteration 87

Universities 14, 15, 36, 51, 57, 73,
101, 104
USSR 15, 45, 46, 87, 88, 99, 100, 124,
125

Yearbooks 49

Zoology 128